D1741365

FREED FOR FREEDOM

STUDIES IN GALATIANS

By Edward C. Wharton

ISBN: 978-0-89098-354-6

Cover design by Jonathan Edelhuber.

Contents

PART THREE: PRACTICAL ARGUMENT
Galatians 5:1—6:18

Dedication

To Pam and Teri.
My two precious daughters who have chosen the freedom
that is in Christ our Lord.

Introduction

Galatians is one of the most powerful letters penned by the apostle Paul. It is a succinct abbreviation of the book of Romans, but comes in smaller bites that are more easily digested. Having said that I would caution against thinking that smaller bites means less important, or not as powerful. On the contrary, the arguments are much more compact, and the punch, in some respects, even more powerful. This is especially true with regard to legalism, both ancient and modern, to which the Galatian letter addresses itself.

Perhaps a clarification about legalism is in order. Too often there has been a misunderstanding of what legalism actually is. Consequently it continues to lurk as a threat to God's people. Legalism is not law keeping, it is law depending. Attempting to do away with keeping Christ's commandments as requisite to salvation by claiming that we are not justified by law, and to say we do not have to obey the law, is to say two very different things. Paul never does away with law keeping; he does away with law depending. Salvation is by atonement (what Christ does for me), not by attainment (what I do for myself).

The message contained in *Freed for Freedom*, as an exposition of Galatians, will be relevant to anyone who finds himself in an extreme position in the body of Christ (whether the rigid right or the loose left). Wharton asks us to do some serious spiritual probing to lead us to a balanced view of the freedom we find in Christ—a freedom that does not play down the importance of obedience. But for anyone who trusts in his obedience to make him right with God, Wharton's exposition of the Galatian letter is devastating.

This book should be useful as a Bible class tool in any adult Bible class in the local church. It will cause us to re-evaluate the ground on which we stand before Christ, and to appreciate what was accomplished at the cross.

Secondly, the book should be used as a tool for evangelism. It explains the balance between the grace of God and an obedience of faith.

Freed For Freedom provides a needed air of assurance that salvation is granted to faith-driven people who, in humble obedience, place their trust in Christ for deliverance and preservation.

Edward P. Myers, Ph.D.
Professor of Bible and Christian Doctrine
Harding University
College of Bible and Religion
Searcy, Arkansas

Preface

Christianity has ever been challenged to move its compass to the right or to the left of its original apostolic setting. Early Christian converts sailed in the crosswinds of a theological tempest that has since proved to be an unrelenting storm of conflict between the liberal left and the legalistic right for control of the church. Paul expresses his own tortured anxiety over the vulnerability of the newly formed churches to such extremes of Christian interpretation when he said "there is the daily pressure on me of concern for all the churches" (2 Corinthians 11:28).

These challenges originated from sources within and without those early churches. From without came the Gentile philosophers substituting human wisdom for God's divine revelation, a revelation that had reached its sufficiency and finality in the historical Christ and in the inspired proclamation of the gospel. From within came the Jewish legalists binding the law of Moses on Christian Gentiles as a necessary element for their salvation.

While other New Testament writings address the challenge of liberalism, Galatians deals with the human extremes of legalism and the divine principles of continuous freedom from sin. Paul writes that Christians have been freed for freedom (Galatians 5:1). Christ set us free from sin to remain free from sin in spite of our inveterate human proneness to sin (1 John 1:10; cf. 1 Kings 8:46; 2 Chronicles 6:36; Psalm 130:3, 4; 143:2). Even now there exists within the body of Christ a legalism that claims faith in Christ, but denies to the faithful Christian the confidence of continuous freedom from his sinful imperfections and the joy and dynamic motivation to faithful Christian living that issues from the ongoing nature of justification by faith. At the same time there is a fairly large segment of sincere believers in Christ who deny the possibility that the Christian can, through legalism or any other means, lose his salvation. These maintain that while the Galatians would return to bondage by accepting the law of Moses (Galatians 4:8-10; 5:1) they would not return to their former bondage to sin. They maintain that this bondage is drudgery to law keeping and mere bondage to the spiritual immaturity under which the law kept the Jews. But the bondage of the Galatian letter is far more serious than mere slavery to the ritual of law, or even hindrance to spiritual growth. Paul writes that false teachers would spy out the freedom we have in Christ and bring us into bondage (Galatians 2:4). In Galatians Paul sets freedom in contrast to bondage. Before Paul came with the gospel the Galatians were held in bondage to sin and death from which their pagan idolatry could not set them free. When they heard the gospel as preached by Paul, they believed it, obeyed it, and were made free. This freedom we have in Christ is freedom from bondage to sin, death, and hell. The bondage of which Paul speaks in Galatians is the bondage from which Christ set us free when He went in our place to the cross (Galatians 3:13). The bondage to which we can return through legal law is the bondage from which Christ set us free when by faith we were baptized into Him.

The message of Galatians is one of life and death. The gospel preached to the Galatians is that through the cross sinners can by faith in Christ be freed from sin, and by faithfulness (not sinlessness) remain free from sin and have peace with God. At the same time, the principle teaching of the message of Galatians is that through legal law, or some other legalism, those who have been justified by faith in Christ can nevertheless forfeit their sonship, their freedom from sin, and return to the bondage of eternal condemnation. Nothing less than this constitutes the seriousness of the Galatian letter.

But while faithful Christians are not equated with perfectly sinless Christians, Paul writes that living the crucified life is requisite to receiving mercy from God and to result in peace with God (Galatians 6:14-16). Paul teaches that neither the cost of our salvation as paid by Christ at the cross nor the cost to us of walking by the Spirit's guidance in a radical lifestyle reversal is cheap.

Galatians is much more than an exposé of the error of justification by the law of Moses. It is a defense of the divine principle of justification by faith in Christ against the legalistic error of salvation by works of legal law.

It is this latter challenge of legalism, its ancient and modern manifestations and its divine solution, that we consider in this study of Galatians.

Ed Wharton
September, 1994

Chapter One
Introducing Galatians

I. Galatians Is Relevant

The Galatians message is in touch with our basic human need to have a spiritually secure and emotionally stable relationship with God. Christians whose hearts are not truly secure in their salvation are probably walking a tightrope between the world and faithful service to Christ. It is difficult to be faithfully committed when one is not sure of his salvation. To remain faithful, to grow, and to bear fruit, we need the assurance that God still loves us and by His grace still accepts us, though as yet we still have a proneness to sin. Faithful Christian experience will testify that such confidence invariably issues in an ever increasing faithfulness that grows not out of fear, but out of a genuine gratitude for the unspeakable gift of His Son Jesus Christ. The lost can be more easily won to Christ and Christians will grow increasingly more faithful and joyous when they learn from Scripture that they can be confident of their salvation. Galatians is the message that faithful, though imperfect, Christians are free from condemnation because of Christ's work on the cross. We are free not only from the guilt and penalty of sin, but from law systems of a condemning legal nature.

In Galatians Paul's principal subject matter is justification by faith in Christ. Its modern relevance is highlighted by contrasting man's characteristic disposition toward self-justification to gain a right standing with God to the impotence of attempting to achieve that right standing through keeping a law system like the law of Moses. In Galatians, salvation emerges as the gracious result of divine atonement rather than the outcome of human attainment.

Galatians elaborates two fundamental principles of freedom from sin that can secure the faithful Christian's confidence that he has a right standing with God even though he is not sinless. First, our freedom is through justification by our faith in Christ. Paul teaches by both historical precedent (3:6, 7) and by divine promise (3:8, 9) that faith in the Lord has always been God's chosen means of salvation. Second, Paul elaborates the principle of the utter impossibility of justification by any legal system, and on that ground therefore reasons that justification cannot come through the legal system of Moses' law (2:16; 3:10-12; 4:21-31). For since justification is by faith it cannot be by law, for, as the law itself says, "The righteous shall live by his faith" (Habakkuk 2:4), and Paul affirms that "the Law is not of faith" (3:12). Because of false teaching in the Galatian churches, that circumcision and keeping the law of Moses were necessary for salvation, Paul has to defend the first principle, justification by faith in Christ, calling it "the truth of the gospel" (2:5, 14) and thus making a distinction between it and the teaching of recent interlopers which was not gospel truth. But coming out of a pagan background of legalism—of attempting to earn salvation by achieving righteousness through good works, Paul had to expose the error of the false teachers who contradicted the second principle: the impossibility of salvation through a system of law like the law of Moses. This clarification needs to be carefully explained to the church today.

II. The Abiding Value of the Galatian Message

It should be emphasized that the message of Galatians is more than a mere refutation of justification by the law of Moses. It is in principle a closely reasoned statement that God's new covenant provision of justification by grace through faith in Christ is totally sufficient to save sinful humanity and entirely independent of human merit by works of any sort under any system. The abiding value of the Galatian message is

A. That God's system of justification by faith in Christ is sufficient for the salvation of all sinners (3:6-9).

B. That faithful Christians, while imperfect, are free from the guilt of sin and the condemnation of law (5:1, 13; 6:14-16). John agrees when he says, "but if we walk in the Light (speaking of faithful Christians)...the blood of Jesus His Son cleanses us from all sin" (1 John 1:7). If walking in the light were sinless perfection, what sin would there be for the blood to cleanse us from?

C. That it is utterly impossible for human flesh to achieve salvation by merit through mere law keeping (2:15, 16; 3:11). To believe justification can be merited by observing a codified system of law is to count the grace of God and the cross of Christ as non essentials (2:21); a repudiation of the gospel message and the Christian faith.

D. That a principle inherent in the nature of any legal law, like the law of Moses, is the condemnation of the violator at the first infraction (3:10). This was one of Paul's principal strategies in answering the law binders, and in educating the Galatian Christians to the pernicious error of such legalism.

E. For a Christian to trust in his own human ability (Paul's reference to "flesh") to be right with God merely by keeping commandments of the new covenant, without trusting in Christ as sin-offering, is to fall from saving grace; the natural consequence of a misplaced faith in something or someone other than Christ (2:20; 5:1-4).

III. Historical Background

A. PAUL ESTABLISHED THE GALATIAN CHURCHES (1:8, 9; 4:11-16).

In the course of his letter Paul reminds the Galatians of the extreme joy they experienced and of the uncommon reverence and gratitude they felt for him when he originally preached the gospel to them (4:13-15). This accounts for his deep paternal feeling for them, calling them "my children," and the fatherly perplexity he was experiencing over their recent engagement with Judaistic teaching (4:19, 20).

B. IDENTIFYING THE GALATIANS

Paul addressed this letter to "the churches of Galatia"(1:2). Who these particular Galatians were and where they were located may yet be a matter of investigation for some. But the evidence is very strong that these "churches of Galatia" are the converts of Paul's first missonary journey as recorded in Acts 13-14. Whether they were located in the more northerly territory of the original kingdom of Galatia or in the more southerly locale of the Roman province of Galatia, which included the former kingdom and much additional territory, is an ongoing debate. But if the "Galatia" of "the churches of Galatia" (1:2) are identified with the Galatians to the south, they would surely be the churches Paul and Barnabas established in their first evangelistic tour to that region. Most American and British scholarship hold this view.[1] This is the view advanced in this study.

IV. Important Terms

It is characteristic of the Bible writers to use significant terms without defining them. Such terms as *justification, reconciliation, sin,* and *gospel* are used in Scripture with an apparent assumption that the reader would understand them. This leaves the impression that at the time of the writing such words were not necessarily religious in meaning, but were common vernacular words used on the street. However, some of these words have since been taken to mean less, or more, or even to have another meaning than the one intended by the writer and consequently require some degree of definition.

There are also those words that are not Bible words, but that express significant biblical subject matter, like *legalism* and *Judaizer*. These, too, must be defined for conventional meaning.

The following terms and their definitions are significant to a common understanding of the Galatian message.

A. LAW—a system of regulation, a rule of conduct, principle, norm.

   1. **Law without the definite article**. This usage in Galatians seems to indicate the law principle in contrast to specifying a particular law. See Galatians 2:16, 19, 21; 3:2, 5, 10a, 11, etc. where the definite article does not appear in the manuscripts before the word *law*. In these statements Paul does not seem to be referring specifically to the law of Moses, but to the general principle of law, or legal jurisprudence. Hence a legal system as distinct from "*the* law of Christ" (Galatians 6:2), "*the* law of faith" (Romans 3:27), or "*the* law of liberty" (James 1:25). Herein seems to reveal Paul's strategy to expose the error of the legalism at Galatia: inasmuch as man cannot be justified by any

system of law, therefore no one can be justified by the Mosaic system of law.

2. **Law and the definite article**. The definite article *the* preceding the word *law* usually focuses attention on a specific law as distinguished from a general reference to the law principle. For an illustration, in James 1:25 "*the* perfect law, *the* law of liberty" is specified by the use of the definite article. So also Paul in Galatians specifies the law of Moses by the use of the definite article, "For as many as are of the works of the Law are under a curse; for it is written, [now notice the use of the definite article in reference to the law of Moses] 'CURSED IS EVERYONE WHO DOES NOT ABIDE BY ALL THINGS WRITTEN IN THE BOOK OF THE LAW, TO PERFORM THEM'....However, the Law is not of faith....Christ redeemed us from the curse of the Law....Why the Law then? It was added because of transgressions....Is the Law then contrary to the promises of God?....Tell me, you who want to be under law, do you not listen to the law?....And I testify again to every man who receives circumcision, that he is under obligation to keep the whole Law" (Galatians 3:10, 12, 13, 19, 21; 4:21; 5:3).

3. **The strategic use and non-use of the definite article with the word *law* in Galatians.** Twice in Galatians 3:10-12 Paul reasons that what is true regarding the nature of legal systems of law must be true of the law of Moses since Moses' law is a legal system. It seems reasonable from the original language that in this particular statement Paul appeals to the law principle, rather than specifically to the law of Moses by referring twice to "law" without the definite article. First, the original language states that law curses the imperfect observer, "For as many as are of works of Law are under a curse" (3:10). Then he reasons that it is not in the nature of law to justify, for, "no man is justified by the law before God" (3:11, ASV). At the same time, in the same statements, he applies the principle of the inability of law to justify to the law of Moses by the conspicuous use of the definite article: "for it is written, Cursed is every one who continueth not in all

things that are written in the book of *the* law, to do them" (3:10, ASV), and, "The righteous shall live by faith; and *the* law is not of faith" (3:11, 12, ASV).

It seems that Paul's use and non-use of the definite article with the word *law* in Galatians is a strategy to explain that what is true regarding the principle of law is true regarding the law of Moses.

4. **The threefold nature of law**. In Romans, after Paul teaches that as a free gift God's own righteousness is reckoned to our faith in Christ (Romans 3:21-26), he asks, "Where then is boasting? It is excluded. By what kind of law? Of works? No, but by a law of faith" (Romans 3:27). Paul carefully distinguishes between a law of works and a law of faith and teaches that we are justified by a law of faith. When Paul therefore writes, "if you are led by the Spirit, you are not under law," we must not interpret that to mean that Christians are without any kind of law. We must instead try to determine what *kind* of law is under consideration.

Paul teaches that the threefold nature of a legal law, like the law of Moses, (1) requires sinless observance (Galatians 3:12, quoting Leviticus 18:5), (2) condemns the violator at the first infraction (Galatians 3:10, quoting Deuteronomy 27:26), and (3) by its nature therefore cannot justify the sinner (Galatians 3:11, quoting Habakkuk 2:4). This may be the single most informative statement Paul makes in all his letters as to why men cannot be justified by any legal system and therefore why the Galatians could not be justified by the law of Moses.

Paul explains that the very nature of any legal system is to condemn the violator. This is why Paul refers to the law of Moses as a "ministration of condemnation" (2 Corinthians 3:9, ASV), and a "ministration of death" (2 Corinthians 3:7, ASV). Inasmuch as all have sinned (Romans 3:23), the law that requires sinless perfection can only condemn the sinner. The Mosaic law was holy, righteous, and good (Romans 7:12), but it could not give life to the transgressor, only condemnation and death.

The significance of the nature of legal systems to Paul's proposition in Galatians cannot be overstated. Some important observations for our current needs can be drawn from this ground.

a. **The law of Christ is not a legal system of law.** Christ's new law of faith allows us to be justified, accounted as righteous. This is the most remarkable thing that sinful ears have ever heard. Sinners, Paul says, when committed to the pattern of gospel teaching, are at the point of baptism, "freed from sin" (Romans 6:1-7, 17, 18). Furthermore, he writes that God condemns the sin of the Christian who faithfully walks by the Spirit and not by trust in one's own flesh power (Romans 8:1-4). This is why James can speak of the new covenant as "the law of liberty" (James 1:25), and how Paul can say to faithful Christians, "It was *for* freedom that Christ set us free; therefore keep standing firm" (Galatians 5:1). At baptism alien sinners have been freed from the guilt and the penalty of their past sins for continual freedom from the guilt and penalty of their future sins. Having been freed from sin by obedience of faith in Christ, we have but to "*stand fast*" by a continual obedience of faith, and we will continually be kept free from the guilt of our future sinful imperfections.

John said the same thing: "But if we walk in the light, as he is in the light, we have fellowship one with another, and the blood of Jesus his Son cleanseth us from all sin" (1 John 1:7, ASV). Walking in the light, or standing fast, is obedience of faith. But it cannot mean sinless perfection as required under a legal system, for then there would be no sin from which the blood continually cleanses us. Among John's closing encouragements to be faithful is his great motivational statement that Christ will not allow the evil one to "touch" those who have renounced the sinner's lifestyle: "We know that no one who is born of God sins; but He who was born of God keeps him, and the evil one does not touch him" (1 John 5:18). The original language makes it clear that John's "*no one who is born of God sins"* means that no true Christian continues to practice sin. Hence the rendering of the New International Version: "We know that anyone born of God does not continue to sin; the one who was born of God keeps him safe, and the evil one cannot harm him."

The new law of Christ is not a legal system that condemns at the first infraction; it is a law of faith by which we are justified. It is a law that brings life and glorious liberty to those whose faithful trust is in Christ.

b. **The law of Christ does not condemn those under it.**

There is therefore now no condemnation to them that are in Christ Jesus. For the law of the Spirit of life in Christ Jesus made me free from the law of sin and of death. For what the law could not do, in that it was weak through the flesh, God, sending his own Son in the likeness of sinful flesh and for sin, condemned sin in the flesh (Romans 8:1-3, ASV).

While sinners outside of Christ are condemned by the law (Romans 3:19, 20), God condemns the sins of those who are in Christ. The reason Paul gives is that the law of the Spirit, which brings life, makes us free from the law that brings death to sinners outside of Christ. The law of sin and death—not the law of Moses—was pronounced by God in the Garden when He said, "In the day thou eatest thereof thou shalt surely die*"* (Genesis 2:17, ASV), and was enacted with the sin of Adam. He sinned, and he died, being separated from God. That law is still operative today. Men still sin and die. But those in Christ have been freed from the law of sin and death—from the law which separates men from God when they sin. Imperfect Christians, who are ordering their lives after the law of Christ due to faith in him, are not condemned for their sins, for God condemns their sins. He continually cleanses them from all sin. He reckons their faith in Christ for righteousness. Christians have been freed from sin for freedom from sin. Hence, *"*It was *for* freedom that Christ *set* us free" (Galatians 5:1).

It should be pointed out that this freedom from condemnation by the law of sin and death is not unconditional. The condition is faith in Christ as sin-offering that leads the trusting repentant sinner to obedience. Hence, "obedience of faith" (Romans 16:26) includes both the alien sinner's initial act of faith in Christ to repent and be immersed for remission of sins (Acts 2:38), and then to follow Christ by standing fast, by walking in the light. Or as Paul elaborates, God through Christ "condemned sin in the flesh, so that the requirement of the Law might be fulfilled in us, who do not walk according to the flesh but according to the Spirit" (Romans 8:3, 4). The requirement of the law of Moses is sinless perfection, which is the requirement of any legal law. But though all men sin, Christians included, this requirement of sinless perfection is nevertheless fulfilled in behalf of Christians whose faith in Christ leads them to walk, not by trusting in the power of human flesh to achieve a right standing with God, but by the Spirit's law of faith in Christ for continual justification.

c. **By distinguishing between the law of Moses as a law of works, which is a legal law, and the law of Christ as a law of faith, which is not a legal law**, the confusion stemming from some of Paul's seeming statements of contradiction are clarified—namely, Paul's statement to the Romans that "sin shall not have dominion over you, for you are not under law, but under grace" (Romans 6:14). At the same time he writes to the Corinthians that we are not "without law to God, but under law to Christ" (1 Corinthians 9:21, ASV). Notice the paradox:

Not under law, Romans 6:14

Under law to Christ, 1 Corinthians 9:21

The question naturally rises, How one can be under law and not under law at the same time? The question is answered when we understand that Paul is speaking of different kinds of laws. We are not under a legal system like Moses' law

(Romans 6:14), which is Paul's subject in Romans, and are therefore not condemned by it when we sin. But we are under the law of Christ and are expected to walk by it as our lifestyle (1 Corinthians 9:21).

Again Paul writes in the original language, "But if you are led by the Spirit, you are not under Law," (Galatians 5:18). However, James says, "But one who looks intently at the perfect law, the law of liberty, and abides by it...this man will be blessed in what he does" (James 1:25). Notice again the paradox:

Not under law, Galatians 5:18

Must continue in the perfect law of liberty, James 1:25

It should be obvious that Paul and James are speaking of two different kinds of laws. As noted above there is a law of works which is a legal law, and there is the law of faith which is not a legal law (Romans 3:27). If we walk by the Spirit, that is, obey the Spirit's teachings by rendering an obedience of faith in Christ under the law of liberty, we will not be led into a system of law that condemns when we sin.

d. **The threefold nature of law contradicts the position of legalists that one is justified by law keeping**.

Inasmuch as it is the very nature of law to condemn the violator, it is therefore quite impossible for law to justify the violator. Law cannot justify the man it condemns. This truth stands in opposition to the position of Judaizers, whether ancient or modern, that justification can be attained by law keeping.

The doctrine of the false teachers at Galatia was that the law of Moses was necessary for salvation. This is clearly stated at Antioch of Syria immediately following Paul's first missionary journey into the Galatian regions: "Some men came down from Judea and began teaching the brethren, 'Unless you are circumcised according to the custom of Moses, you cannot be saved'" (Acts 15:1). Later at Jerusalem when the apostles gathered with the church to consider this matter, Luke writes, "But some of the sect of the Pharisees who had believed stood up saying, 'It is necessary to circumcise them, and to direct them to observe the Law of Moses'" (Acts 15:5). Paul's Galatian letter also reveals this same legalism as the doctrine of the troublemakers at Galatia (Galatians 2:3, 4, 16, 21; 3:2, 21; 4:4, 5, 9-11, 21-31; 5:2-4, 18; 6:12, 13). This doctrine exposes the fundamental error of the Galatian legalists: they understood neither the condemning nature of the law of Moses, nor the sufficiency of the gospel to justify the sinner. Had they understood the nature of the gospel message—justification by God's grace through our faith in Christ—they would have known that they had no need for the law of Moses, nor for any addendum to the gospel. Since Christ's work at the cross is sufficient to satisfy God for all our sins, and since our faith in Christ is reckoned for righteousness, there is no more to be done to give alien sinners and imperfect Christians a right standing with God. And had they understood the nature of the law, that it could only condemn the sinner, they would not have taught that it could save the sinner.

The law of faith is not a legal system that requires perfection and condemns its violators, but it requires faith in Christ, which God reckons for righteousness, and a genuine intent to observe the Lord's commandments (Galatians 6:14-16). Thus Paul's original proclamation of the gospel to the Galatians at Antioch of Pisidia was, "Therefore let it be known to you, brethren, that through Him forgiveness of sins is proclaimed to you, and through Him everyone who believes is freed [justified] from all things, from which you could not be freed [justified] through the Law of Moses" (Acts 13:38, 39). Thank God that justification is by faith in Christ. Praise God for such a law that liberates rather than condemns the violator.

B. JUSTIFICATION—From the verb to justify, meaning to declare one righteous. Justification, as used by Paul, refers to the right standing one has before God due to the work of Christ in His death and resurrection (Romans 4:25; 5:16, 18). "It is a term of ethical relationship, not ethical quality, and signifies the footing on which one is set towards another, not the character imparted to one."[2]

Speaking of the importance of the term Leon Morris writes,

> He who would expound justification is confronted with eighty-one occurrences of the adjective *dikaios*, ninety-two of the noun *dikaiosune*, two of the noun *dikaiosis*, thirty-nine of the verb *dikaioo*, ten of the noun *dikaioma*, and five of the adverb *dikaios*...the bare enumeration of the number of passages to be considered indicates that we are here dealing with a conception of great importance.[3]

Justification is the merciful act of God in behalf of the sinner. On the divine ground of Christ's cross and by the human means of faith in Christ, God himself declares the sinner justified, He has accounted his faith for righteousness.

1. **The meaning of justification in courts of law**. Justification in a legal sense refers to the act of declaring one just or free of guilt. The justified one is vindicated, or acquitted of a crime. The accused has been found not guilty, innocent of wrongdoing. The justified man then, in our current vernacular, is an innocent man. Generally, then, "The term is used to excuse action or to prove one was right in acting as he did, to vindicate himself either in the eyes of man or of the law. A person may say, 'The man accused of murder did not commit murder. He was "justified" in killing the intruder because he acted in self-defense.'"[4] But we should not be misled into thinking that this is the way the term is used in Scripture regarding our salvation from sin.

2. **Paul's meaning of justification**. The terms *justification* and *justify* are used by Paul in a special biblical and judicial sense meaning to declare or to account the sinful man as righteous. The sinner is in fact not righteous, nor is he made righteous; he is as guilty as sin. But according to Paul, God accepts him and looks upon him as *if* he were righteous because of his faith in the atoning work of Christ. As Leon Morris observes, "Men are justified on Paul's view not on account of any merit of their own,

potential or actual, but only on account of Christ's work and of their faith."[5]

In the following Scriptures Paul speaks of justification as an act of God Himself wherein the sinner is accounted righteous before God, though in fact he is not righteous, and where the sinner's faith is reckoned for righteousness.

a. **Galatians 3:6-8.** Abraham is the classic example of faith as the means of our own justification. On the occasion when God promised Abraham that he would have descendants as the stars of heaven (Genesis 15:6) Abraham believed God, and Moses writes that "it [his belief] was reckoned to him as righteousness." Paul quotes this in Galatians 3:6-8 and says that God further promised to Abraham in Genesis 12:3 that He would justify all men in the same way, by faith, "*even as*" He justified Abraham.

Paul's point is that faith is the means of our justification even as faith was the means of Abraham's justification. But *our* point is that in Paul's reasoning he equates the justification of Abraham as being reckoned as righteous.

b. **Romans 4:5-8.** Paul also relates the account of David's justification after his adulterous sin with Bathsheba. He quotes David's own words (Psalm 32:1, 2), traditionally written after his justification, as authority for the statement that David's belief was reckoned for righteousness:

But to the one who does not work, but believes in Him who justifies the ungodly, his faith is credited as righteousness, just as David also speaks of the blessing on the man to whom God credits righteousness apart from works: "Blessed are those whose lawless deeds have been forgiven, and whose sins have been covered. Blessed is the man whose sin the Lord will not take into account" (Romans 4:5-8).

While David was justified *under* the law, he was not justified *by* the law. Paul's point is that we are justified by faith "just as David" was. Not only was David's faith accounted as righteousness, but his sin was not counted against him. Such is the incomparable blessing of the justified then and now.

God intruded Himself into history from the beginning for our sakes. He justly "passed over the sins previously committed" (Romans 3:25), knowing from the beginning that He would become one of us in the person of Christ, to become sin-offering, savior, and advocate. Without God's inexpressible love, without Christ and Calvary, without the gospel to produce saving faith, and without God's merciful willingness to account that faith for righteousness, sinful fallen man would simply be without hope and without God in the world. Praise God for His unspeakable gift!

C. LEGALISM.

1. **A theological error**. Legalism is not a Bible term, but it is a Bible subject. As a theological term *legalism* can be defined as a code of deeds and observances as a means of justification. What is "a code of deeds and observances" but a law? Thus legalism by definition claims that law is a means of justification. However, Paul states that is a theological error. At Antioch he publically reminds Peter, who pretended that the law was necessary (Galatians 2:11-13), that the reason both of them believed on Christ for justification was precisely because no man can be justified by the works of the law, and that Peter knew it:

   We are Jews by nature and not sinners from among the Gentiles; nevertheless knowing that a man is not justified by the works of the Law but through faith in Christ Jesus, even we have believed in Christ Jesus, so that we may be justified by faith in Christ and not by the works of the Law; since by the works of the Law no flesh will be justified (Galatians 2:15, 16).

   Legalism as a theology of salvation by law keeping must be understood today as a logical contradiction of both the nature of law and the apostle's pronouncement that no man can be justified by the works of a legal system. Legalism understands neither the condemning nature of law nor the gospel of salvation by grace through faith in Christ as sin-offering. As a theology, legalism is a lie inasmuch as it deceives the very ones subscribing to it into thinking they can be saved merely by attempting to keep the law when Scripture plainly states it is not so. Legalism also denies what Scripture affirms, that for Christians not all sin leads to death (1 John 5:16, 17). Rather, if we continue to walk in the light, that is, if we obediently practice righteousness and trust in Christ as sin-offering, not in our walking, the blood of Christ will continue to cleanse us from all sin (1 John 1:7).

2. **Legalism identifies with the theology of the Pharisees**. While not a Bible word, *legalism* is identified with the erroneous theology of the Pharisees, as well as with that doctrine taught at Antioch, Jerusalem, and Galatia. Legalism is the "bootstrap" method of self-effort that places trust in mere human flesh to keep enough commandments to merit a right standing with God. The New Testament reveals it as a pernicious teaching to be vigorously opposed. Jesus dealt with it when He spoke of those "who trusted in themselves that they were righteous" (Luke 18:9-14). Phariseeism was not dead in the early church. To the extent that legalism is in the body of Christ today, Phariseeism still lives and threatens the salvation and the unity of God's precious people. The hope of the gospel is not only a *desire* to be eternally saved, but a legitimate *expectation* that eternal salvation is assured to the faithful Christian. Legalism, by its nature, cancels out the Christian's assurance and puts in its place an "I'll just have to wait and see what God decides at judgment" attitude.

When tempted to sin, legalism offers no divine strength to resist. For his confidence for justification, like the Pharisee in Jesus' parable, is not in Christ as sin-offering whom God accepts on our behalf to forgive, but in his own human ability to keep enough commandments to satisfy God. He does not operate according to gospel knowledge inasmuch as he is not knowledgeable of God's righteousness, which once again we stress, is justification by faith in Christ. As Paul wrote of Christ to the Corinthians, God made Christ to be our righteousness (1 Corinthians 1:30). Being ignorant of that good news message the legalist seeks to establish his own righteousness merely by keeping commandments, whether as the Pharisee under the Law, or the Christian under the law of liberty. But by the nature of legalism one can never know if he has done enough. This begets the gnawing fear that one cannot be confident of his salvation. Thus under legalism only frustration and fear follow in its wake.

3. **The two faces of legalism**. By its nature legalism manifests itself in two forms, arrogance and fear. Those who put their trust for salvation in themselves to keep God's commandments best they can set themselves forth as a standard against which others are measured. This is the meaning of the term "self-righteous," with emphasis on "self." Hence, Jesus said they arrogantly "viewed others with contempt." He then graphically illustrates legalism by the self-righteous Pharisee who, though himself a sinner, trusted in himself that by keeping certain aspects of the law was therefore righteous before God. Then turning from the implicit fact of his own sin, which he patently refused to admit, he contemptuously scorned his Jewish brother, the publican, who candidly admitted his sinfulness, expressed deep and sincere repentance, and, being a covenant Israelite, put his trust in a merciful God to forgive him at the moment of supplication (Luke 18:9-14). Christ then pronounced that the trusting publican went down to his house justified rather than the legalistic Pharisee. Thus Christ defines a legalist as one who "exalts himself" by trusting in mere commandment keeping as if keeping some commandments would exonerate him from the guilt of having transgressed other commandments. By this means he trusts in himself for a right relationship with God.

This idea is resident within the body of Christ today, and feeds the insidious fear of some otherwise very conscientious and obedient Christians that they simply cannot know if they have done enough to be saved. They believe Jesus is Lord, that the Bible is the Word of God, that they must keep the commandments of Christ as the new way of life. But legalism's trust is in self to be good enough, not in Christ as sin-offering and propitiation to account our accompanying faith in Christ for righteousness. This misconception of Christianity causes some to resign themselves in despair to the gnawing uncertainty of their eternal future. They want to live for Christ but do not experience the motivating joy of their salvation or the confidence of a secure relationship with a gracious and forgiving Father. Affected by legalism, many despair that Christianity is too hard and in frustration no longer feel they can "hold out." Legalism makes question marks rather than exclamation points. With an attitude of "what's the use," sincere Christians can become vulnerable to trials rather than motivated to resist them and overcome them by an assured confidence that through faith in Christ we can continue to have fellowship with God. Others in disillusionment or bitterness abandon the faith. Legalism does not view Christianity as good news. In a word, legalism simply does not understand God's good news message of justification by an obedience of faith in Christ.

4. **Legalism today**. The current dilemma with Christians, as in the Galatian churches, is trusting in the wrong person or the wrong thing for salvation. The Galatians were being duped into turning their faith inward upon themselves to meet the law's perfect requirement (Galatians 3:3), and away from Christ who promises to make propitiation for sinful imperfections: "Therefore, He had to be made like his brethren in all things, so that he might become a merciful and faithful high priest in things pertaining to God, to make propitiation for the sins of the people" (Hebrews 2:17). Clearly, Christ is our propitiation, that is, our satisfaction before God. At the cross He satisfied God's justice for the sins of His people, the church. Oh, they believe Jesus is Lord. But is trust *in Him*, that what He accomplished at the cross is enough to guarantee to the trusting Christian that he is eternally secure? For Christians to attempt to be justified merely by keeping commandments is equal to trusting in the power of one's own ability to make atonement for his own sins. Trust in self abandons trust in Christ. Trust in Christ as sin-offering at the

moment that faith leads to obedience, whether for the alien sinner at baptism or for the Christian praying for forgiveness, is essential for justification. If justification is by mere commandment keeping without conscientiously trusting in Christ as the One who is satisfying God's justice, then Christ died for nothing. Paul so taught when he said, "If righteousness comes through the Law, then Christ died needlessly" (Galatians 2:21). The law of Moses was in place fifteen hundred years before Christ. That law was perfect (Psalm 19:7). If justification were by that law, or if any such law existed prior to or since Christ, by which sinners could be justified, then Christ died for nothing. If we could make ourselves perfect by keeping that perfect law then why would Jesus have to die to make us perfect? Theologically and practically speaking, any so-called system of justification apart from obedience of faith in Christ necessarily wipes out the gospel and makes the cross of Christ a meaningless sentiment.

Paul teaches that sinful man is helpless without help from God. He explains that in Christ's dying He did for us what we cannot do for ourselves merely through attempting to keep God's righteous commandments (Galatians 3:13). He further explained that our faith must be *in Christ* to be reckoned for righteousness (Galatians 2:16). The difference, then, between legalism and justification by faith is the difference in the objects of our trust for justification. We must keep the commandments as an expression of our faith in Christ and repentance from sin. But our faith must be *in Christ*, not our commandment keeping. Saving faith is not in Christ's mother, nor in any other. Certainly not in self. Either we trust in our own works (which is tantamount to trusting in ourselves to do those works), or we trust in Christ's atoning sacrifice at Calvary which alone satisfies God for our sins.

A great part of the problem today that produces so much uncertainty about our eternal salvation lies in confusing our obedience of faith *in* Christ with faith in our obedience *to* Christ.

The first strengthens; the other frustrates. The gospel puts faith in Christ; legalism puts faith in self. The gospel, understood and put into practice, naturally issues in the Christian's gratitude, eager obedience, and joyful confidence. Legalism robs the sincere Christian of the joy of his salvation, and often produces its natural fruit of arrogance and fear, and sadly too often issues in a defeated Christian giving up the fight. God forbid that such morbid results be equated with the fruit of God's good news message.

D. THE GOSPEL

Gospel means good news, glad tidings. It is the good news message from God announcing to lost humanity that He has such an incredible love for us that He became one of us in the person of Christ, by His crucifixion He satisfied the justice of God paying the price for our sin, and that now, sinners though we are, we can be accounted righteous by placing our faith in Christ as sin-offering and Savior. The gospel is God's own good tidings that through Christ we can begin an eternal relationship with God while yet here on earth. For this reason it is called "the gospel of the grace of God" (Acts 20:24), and "the gospel of your salvation" (Ephesians 1:13). In Galatians Paul calls the message of justification by faith in Christ, "the truth of the gospel" (2:5, 14). This is what Paul wrote Galatians to defend.

1. **The Christian's confidence**. The New Testament teaches that while men in sin fear the sentence of the coming great tribunal, Christians can have absolute confidence on the day of judgment: "By this, love is perfected with us, so that we may have confidence in the day of judgment; because as He is, so also are we in this world. There is no fear in love; but perfect love casts out fear, because fear involves punishment, and the one who fears is not perfected in love" (1 John 4:17, 18). Christians who "believe in the name of the son of God" have by that means already entered into an eternal relationship with God. Obedient Christians, however imperfect, can know they have eternal life. As John says, "These things I have written to you who believe in

the name of the Son of God, so that you may know that you have eternal life" (1 John 5:13). Such confidence dispels the fear of punishment for sin and motivates us to a continual obedience of faith in spite of our imperfections (Romans 16:26).

2. **The cross, the divine ground of our justification**. The ground of this confidence is the wonder of the cross of Christ. This is seen in the divine resolution of the dichotomy that exists between the sinfulness of man and God's own extravagant love for man. Since sin brings death to all men, separating them from God (Isaiah 59:2; Romans 6:23), and since all have sinned (Romans 3:23), all men, mature enough to be responsible for their sin, are condemned to death. While the justice of God demands punishment for sin the love of God compels Him to secure our salvation. How can God vindicate His justice and at the same time satisfy His great love? The solution is in the cross of Christ.

The incredibly excessive love of God for sinful humanity compelled Him to go to the cross and suffer the sinner's death penalty (separation from God), to whom the stroke of death is actually due.

But He was pierced through for our transgressions, He was crushed for our iniquities; The chastening for our well-being fell upon Him, And by His scourging we are healed. All of us like sheep have gone astray, Each of us has turned to his own way; But the LORD has caused the iniquity of us all To fall on Him...He was cut off out of the land of the living For the transgression of my people, to whom the stroke was due (Isaiah 53:5, 6, 8).

Thus Christ died the death of a sinner, and as such was separated from God: "My God, my God, why hast thou forsaken me?" (Matthew 27:46, ASV). On the cross He became a curse for us (Galatians 3:13). By His vicarious death He paid the price for our salvation. Such a death on Christ's part was required in the nature of things:

But we do see Him who was made for a little while lower than the angels, namely, Jesus, because of the suffering of death crowned with glory and honor, so that by the grace of God He might taste death for everyone...since the children share in flesh and blood, He Himself likewise also partook of the same, that through death He might render powerless him who had the power of death, that is, the devil (Hebrews 2:9, 14).

Since God's justice allows no alternative, "God demonstrates His own love toward us, in that while we were yet sinners, Christ died for us" (Romans 5:8). The original word *for* is a word of substitution and means "in behalf of." So Paul writes that Christ gave himself *for* our sins, "and the life which I now live in the flesh I live by faith in the Son of God, who loved me and gave Himself up *for* me" (Galatians 1:4; 2:20). And again, "He made Him who knew no sin to be sin on our behalf, so that we might become the righteousness of God in Him" (2 Corinthians 5:21). Christ also became sin-offering (Isaiah 53:10) that He might perfect us, not only until the next time we sin, but forever: "For by one offering he hath perfected for ever them that are sanctified" (Hebrews 10:14, ASV). The incredible wonder of it all is that God offered up His own Son to Himself on our behalf to satisfy His justice in order to justify us. And further, at the cross Christ became our sin-bearer that He might continually bear the guilt of our sins (Isaiah 53:11). Thus John says, "If we walk in the light, as he is in the light, we have fellowship one with another, and the blood of Jesus his Son cleanseth us from all sin" (1 John 1:7, ASV). That's the best news that sinful ears have ever heard.

3. **The gospel message is God's power to save**. The good news message is that God did for man what he cannot do for himself. He paid our sin-debt and now stands ready to free us from the guilt of sin and the condemnation of law if we but respond by trusting Christ to save us and keep us saved. The power of God to save sinners lies in a message of good news that asks for a trusting faith rather than a frustrating legalism that demands an impossible requirement (Romans 1:16, 17). As it is written, "But when the kindness of God our Savior and His love for mankind appeared, He saved us, not on the basis of deeds which we have done in righteousness, but according to His mercy, by the

washing of regeneration and renewing by the Holy Spirit" (Titus 3:4, 5). This is the meaning of Paul's term, "the truth of the gospel," twice used in Galatians in contrast to Jewish legalism (2:5,14). Thank God for His gospel message, for the manifestation of His incredible love, His unspeakable gift!

E. FAITH

The principle that takes its rise from the gospel message is that we are justified by faith in Christ apart from meritorious works of *any* legal system. God's grace is presented in Scripture as the divine ground of our salvation. But while "grace" is mentioned only seven times in Galatians "faith" is mentioned twenty-two times. This manifests Paul's emphasis to his new spiritual children, former pagans immersed in idolatrous legalism, that faith in Christ is the necessary human response for justification.

1. **Faith: the means of our justication**. Galatians clearly teaches that we respond to God's grace for justification by the means of faith in Christ (2:16; 3:8, 9, 11, 14, 22, 24, 26; 5:4, 5). As Paul explains elsewhere, "For by grace you have been saved through faith" (Ephesians 2:8); grace on God's part and faith on ours. Faith is the abiding principle by which men have ever come to a right standing with God. This was the means of justification during the Patriarchal system, which was illustrated in Abraham, as well as the means of David's justification under the Mosaic system (Galatians 3:6) as illustrated in David (Romans 4:1-8). It is the means of justification under the New Covenant. Faith, or belief, has a distinctive definition and a distinctive object.

2. **Saving faith has a distinctive definition**. It is here that we must understand the twofold nature of saving faith. First, faith trusts. In Galatians faith is used of the trust or the confidence the alien sinner must have in the person and work of Christ for justification (2:16; 3:26), and it is used of the Christian's confidence in Christ that strengthens and motivates him to live the Christian life, "...the life which I now live in the flesh I live by faith in the Son of God....For we through the Spirit, by faith, are waiting for the hope of righteousness" (2:20; 5:5). Faith is the act of

trusting or believing, as when "Abraham believed God, and it was reckoned to him as righteousness" (3:6). While saving faith embraces an intellectual belief that Jesus is Lord and Savior, it also embraces a trust in the person and work of Christ as sufficient for our salvation. Faith, then, is that personal belief, that confidence we have in Christ as sin-offering and propitiation which is accounted for righteousness. To believe that Jesus is the resurrected Son of God is one thing, but saving faith must go beyond mere intellectual belief to trust, to the point of having such confidence in Him that we turn our lives over to Him. This is well illustrated in Jairus, a ruler of a Jewish synagogue whose daughter was dying. Jairus' faith went beyond mere intellectual belief that Christ could heal his daughter; he trusted Christ to the point of going to Him and pleading for his daughter's life. But before they arrived at Jairus' house word came to him of his daughter's death. Jesus encouraged him to maintain his trust, "Do not be afraid any longer; only believe, and she will be made well" (Luke 8:50). Jesus asked him to continue in that confidence. James speaks of a doubting kind of faith that prays to God but doubts that He will answer (James 1:5, 6). Saving, prayer-answering faith is more than intellectual belief. It is a trust that generates hope.

Second, saving faith must also act in accordance with God's word. Saving faith obeys. Whether for the alien sinner or the child of God, faith must go beyond mere intellectual belief to what Paul calls, "obedience of faith" (Romans 16:25, 26). In the book of James the Holy Spirit addresses the kind of faith by which men are saved (James 2:14-26). He asks, "What use is it, my brethren, if someone says he has faith, but he has no works? Can that faith save him?" (James 2:14). James is not speaking only of the Christian's faith. He is clearly speaking of the saving faith of "a man." A few verses later he reasons from the kind of faith that Abraham had to a general conclusion for all men, "that *a man* is justified by works, and not by faith alone" (James 2:24). Paul uses the same language with Peter, saying, "*a man* is not justified by the works of the Law but through faith in Christ Jesus" (Galatians 2:16). James, like Paul, though addressing brethren, was speaking of the faith of "a man"—any man. The kind of faith necessary for the ongoing justification of a Christian is the same kind of faith necessary for an alien sinner to be saved.

James answers his own question regarding the saving power of faith without works. He illustrates that such faith is like mere words without benefit to hungry and naked men (James 2:15, 16), and he concludes that "even so faith, if it has no works, is dead, being by itself" (James 2:17). Any man can say he has faith, says James, but saving faith will "show" by his works (James 2:18). It will be seen in the deeds of the true believer. At this point in the text, James illustrates that the kind of faith by which a man is justified is the kind of faith by which Abraham was justified. James teaches that Abraham's faith was "perfected" by his works, and that faith was reckoned for righteousness (James 2:21-23). The kind of faith that saved Abraham obeys God. Abraham's faith was perfected by his obedience, and that faith brought him into a right relationship with God. James then concludes unequivocally that from this historical illustration we are expected to "see that a man is justified by works, and not by faith alone" (James 2:24).

Works of faith are the kind of works that perfect our faith in Christ. We are imperfect and will not be otherwise (1 John 1:9). It is our faith that must be perfected, and that requires the works of faith. We earn nothing through such works. They are but the expressions of our faith in Christ that He will do for us what He said He would when we do what He asks us to. There is no basic difference between James' works of faith, John's walking in the light (1 John 1:7), and Paul's obedience of faith (Romans 1:5; 16:26). There is no doctrinal contradiction between Paul's statement that we are saved by grace through faith and "not as a result of works" (Ephesians 2:8, 9), and James' statement that "a man is justified by works, and not by faith alone." These inspired men are speaking of two different kinds of works. Paul in Ephesians is speaking to former pagans of works of merit; James is speaking of works of faith. When Scripture speaks of justification by faith it infers an obedience of faith.

3. **Faith must have an object**. Faith cannot exist in a vacuum. In order to exist faith must be in something or someone. It must have an object in which to believe. Galatians teaches that the faith that saves must have Christ as the object of that faith. Our faith must be "in Christ." He is the object of our trust.

But when the New Testament speaks of "*the* faith" it does not refer to the act of believing, but rather to the thing believed, the objective Christian faith, as distinguished, for an illustration, from the Islamic faith or the Jewish faith. It is that body of apostolic teaching that makes Christianity what it is. It is the thing preached (Galatians 1:23), the thing believed (Galatians 3:23, 25), the thing obeyed (Acts 6:7), the thing we strive for (Philippians 1:27), the distinctive belief common to "the household of the faith" (Galatians 6:10). Our personal faith, the act of believing and trusting in Christ, is generated by the proclamation of the distinctive Christian faith. Make a distinction between "the faith," the thing believed, and "faith," the act of believing.

F. JUDAIZER—a term not found in the Bible but often used to identify the false teachers at Galatia with their Jewish nationalism and their legalistic doctrine. It is from the Latin *judaizo*, which means "to be or live like a Jew."

It is a religious designation rather than a national description. Their fundamental belief was that Gentiles, even after accepting Jesus as Lord, were expected to live as Jews. The law of Moses was to be observed, not as a matter of custom or culture, but as a necessary supplement to the gospel of grace.[6]

V. THE TROUBLE AT GALATIA AND THE PURPOSE OF THE LETTER

Why the Galatian letter? Paul had hardly left the newly established churches in Galatia when he learned of Jewish legalists who came in among these Gentile churches (1:6), claiming to be Christians (2:4). They taught the Galatians that to maintain their justification the Galatians had to be circumcised and keep the law of Moses (5:2-4). Paul perceived that the legalists' doctrine compromised the cross (2:17, 21), contradicted the gospel of justification by faith (6-8; 2:16; 3:6-9, 21-22, 26), and threatened the very security of the Galatians' salvation (2:11, 18; 4:9, 11; 5:2, 4). To win the Galatians' confidence away from Paul, the Judaizers denied his apostolic authority (1:1), maligned his character as being two-faced (1:10; 4:12-20), and claimed his gospel differed from that of the original apostles (1:11, 12; 2:1-10). Their effectiveness was telling. Not only was Paul's apostleship and character now suspect among the very people whom he had brought out of idolatry into Christ (4:8), but some of them were submitting to Jewish ritual (4:10) and circumcision (5:2, 3).

Paul's purpose in writing the letter was quite understandably to defend the gospel message and to secure his beloved spiritual children in the faith. To do this he had to recapture their confidence in his authority to speak for Christ by defending his divine appointment to the apostleship (1:1—2:21). While on the defensive, Paul was very explicit in his disclosure of the personal, hidden, two-faced motives of these Judaizers who acted out of personal ambition (4:17; 6:13) and offense at the cross of Christ (6:12).

VI. STRUCTURE OF THE LETTER

The Galatian letter is perhaps the most closely reasoned of all of Paul's letters. It is characterized by an economy of words that shows a profound regard for the perceptive and insightful ability of the Galatians, however new to the faith, to plumb the implications of the gospel that were condensed into one tight argument after another. Though written in the passion of an urgent defense, nothing of the letter's content has the telltale marks of having been hastily thrown together. Nothing of the progression of argumentation is even slightly out of sequence. The argumentation begins logically with Paul's historical defense of his apostleship and therefore of his gospel (Chs. 1 and 2).

Next he progresses to the authority of Old Testament Scripture from which he draws testimony that law cannot justify and that men are ever justified by faith. Then he reasons that for these Christian Gentiles to place themselves under the law would be to return to bondage once again even as formerly they were in bondage under idolatry. He concludes this section by correctly allegorizing the account of Hagar and Sarah as historical counterparts of bondage and freedom (Chs. 3 and 4).

Paul finalizes the letter by pointing out some impracticalities of legalism under the law (5:2-12) and the practicality of freedom's walk in brotherly love according to the Spirit's guidance (5:1-6:10). He concludes with a clear contrast of motives between the Judaizers and himself and contrasts their respective objects of glory and confidence: theirs the flesh, his the cross (6:11-18).

Keep in mind that, while the logical structure and content of the letter manifests the keen intellectual skill and insight of the writer, Galatians is not the product of strictly unaided human intellect. Paul's claim at the outset of the letter is that what he preached to the Galatians was by direct revelation from Jesus Christ (1:11, 12). His letters, no less than his preaching, are the result of inspiration by the Holy Spirit. Jesus pledged the Spirit to the guidance of His apostles (John 14:26; 16:13), Paul claimed the same for himself (Ephesians 3:3-5), and Peter pronounced Paul's letters as Scripture (2 Peter 3:15, 16). Galatians is not merely the product of Paul's excellent mind; it is the very Word of God as guided by the Holy Spirit. With this confidence we proceed to the study of the text.

Spiritual Probing
Chapter One

1. Do you believe that a secure relationship with God (being confident of your eternal destiny) is basic to your emotional stability? Do you honestly believe the Bible teaches that we can have a secure relationship with God even though we are not, and will not be, sinless? You don't think God is playing games with us, do you? Do you believe that such a relationship would be less or more of a motivation in living the Christian life as compared to a constant reminder of condemnation for disobedience? Could you, on the basis of Scripture teaching, keep on keeping on if you were not confident of your salvation? Does Galatians 2:19, 20 speak to this matter? If so, how?

2. Can you relate from your own experience how you are much more dynamically motivated to live for Christ through confidence in your salvation than you would be through fear of being lost?

3. From your consideration of the threefold nature of law (a legal system), distinguish the difference between the law of Moses and the Christian law of faith. Of what importance is that difference to you as a faithful but imperfect Christian?

4. Paul states in Romans 7:12 that the law of Moses is holy, righteous, and good. But in 2 Corinthians 3:7, 9 he states that the law of Moses is a letter that condemns, a ministration of death. Why does that good law bring death?

5. Explain Paul's line of reasoning that applies the general principle of legal law to the specific law of Moses as in Galatians 3:10-12.

6. What is it to be justified in a court of law? What is it to be justified by God? Is the Christian's justification the same as a person justified in law courts today? Is it different? How?

7. What is legalism? Is it legalism to insist that Christians are to struggle to obey the commandments of Christ? Explain how legalism as a theology of salvation contradicts both the nature of legal law and Paul's statement that we are not justified by works of law (2:16). In the

light of your answer do you consider the law of Moses legalism? Why or why not? Remember, legalism is not keeping commandments (Matthew 28:20; Hebrews 5:8, 9).

8. Would you say that legalism today is expressed in placing faith in the wrong person? Can you explain?

9. Do you think some very sincere and faithful Christians are not sure about their salvation because they confuse obedience of faith in Christ with faith in their obedience to Christ? Elaborate.

10. What is the good news message of the gospel that Paul defended in the Galatian letter? Do you suppose it may need a defense today?

11. Who are the legalists of today? How are they to be identified?

12. Can a believer be tainted with legalism through a lack of understanding the gospel, yet have his trust in Christ? What do you think is the reason for this?

13. How do you think it would affect those faithful Christians who are tainted with legalism to learn that the law of Christ is not a legal system and that Christ has freed us from sin to remain free from sin?

PART ONE:
HISTORICAL ARGUMENT
Galatians 1:1-2:21

Chapter Two
An Urgent Correspondence
Galatians 1:1-10

The Difference Between a Book and a Letter

The Galatians student needs to keep in mind from the outset the difference between a book and a letter. While Galatians has become one of the "books" of the New Testament, it was written as a letter in the format of first-century letter writing. In books written for publication, the author details all of the background information necessary for a coherent reading of the story. But a letter is usually written in response to an immediate need, either on the part of the writer or the recipients, and the author assumes that his readers are acquainted with the relevant background.

This difference is significant for the Galatians student who would get behind some of Paul's otherwise "orphan" statements by deducting from what he says to why he said it. For an illustration, why does Paul open this letter with a disclaimer regarding his apostleship, stating it was "not sent from men, nor through the agency of man"? What is behind that qualifying statement? Can the answer be implied from what the rest of the letter reveals? When Paul said to the Galatians, "you know that it was because of a bodily illness that I preached the gospel to you the first time" (4:13), does that necessarily imply that Paul had already made a visit or two to these churches? And as this statement also seems to say that Paul's opportunity to preach to these Galatians was serendipitous, rather than the result of an intended preaching campaign, does this imply that the Galatians to whom Paul wrote this letter were not the people of Paul's first missionary journey (Acts 13 and 14), inasmuch as these latter people were sought out intentionally? And is the answer crucial to understanding the message of the text? And what is the message Paul sends with his closing statement, "From now on let no one cause trouble for me, for I bear on my body the brand-marks of Jesus" (6:17)?

Interpreting Galatians is rather like listening to one end of a telephone conversation and attempting to deduce from that what is said at the other end. Such is the difference between a book and a letter, and such is the challenge of the student.

The Difference Between Paul's Correspondence and the Literary Form of Letter Writing in the First Century

This enlightening difference is expressed in the following:

In the Graeco-Roman world private letters averaged close to 90 words in length. Literary letters, such as those by the Roman orator and statesman Cicero and by Seneca the philosopher, averaged around 200 words. Since the usual papyrus sheet measured about 9 1/2 x 11" (approximately the size of our ordinary notebook paper) and could accommodate 150-250 words, depending on the size of writing, most ancient letters occupied no more than one papyrus page. But the average length of Paul's epistles runs to about 1,300 words, ranging from 335 words in Philemon to 7,101 words in Romans. As can be seen, Paul's epistles are several times longer than the average letter of ancient times, so that in a sense Paul invented a new literary form, the epistle—new in its prolongation as a letter, in the theological nature of its contents, and (usually) in the communal nature of its address. From another standpoint, however, Paul's epistles are true letters in that they have genuine and specific addresses, unlike the ancient literary epistles, which were written for general publication, in spite of their artificial addresses.[1]

I. Paul's Introduction, 1:1-5.

Paul, an apostle (not sent from men, nor through the agency of man, but through Jesus Christ and God the Father, who raised Him from the dead), and all the brethren who are with me, To the churches of Galatia: Grace to you and peace from God our Father, and the Lord Jesus Christ, who gave Himself for our sins so that He might rescue us out of this pres-

ent evil age, according to the will of our God and Father, to whom be the glory forevermore. Amen (Galatians 1:1-5).

A. GALATIANS: AN UNUSUAL CORRESPONDENCE

1. **Written in unusually large characters**. An interesting remark at the close of the letter reveals what the Galatians probably saw with astonishment as soon as they unscrolled the letter. Paul writes, "See with what large letters I am writing to you with my own hand" (6:11). Alford's comment "I do not see how it is possible to avoid the inference that these words apply to the whole epistle"[2] is worth considering. His reasoning from the original language is that Paul actually says, "See with what large letters I have written unto you." On the basis of the grammar, Alford reasons that it is quite possible that Paul actually wrote the entire letter himself and that he wrote in unusually large characters.

   Why? There is good reason to believe that Paul had poor eyesight. This seems to be indicated by his statement to the Galatians that "if possible, you would have plucked out your eyes and given them to me*"* (4:15). Comments that this was not to be taken literally, but that it was a common idiom corresponding to a person's generosity, like, "he would give you the shirt off his back," fail to be convincing for lack of evidence. Every other letter of Paul's was actually dictated by him and penned by a secretary. This is illustrated at the end of the Roman letter where the secretary said, "I, Tertius, who write this letter, greet you in the Lord" (16:22). At the end of his letters Paul would write a closing statement authorizing its contents (see Colossians 4:18; 2 Thessalonians 3:17). But if no secretary were available, and the need for the letter was urgent, it would have been necessary for Paul to write the letter himself. But that would place quite a strain on a person with dimmed or diseased eyesight. Hence the oversized letters of Galatians 6:11 would be necessary for such a writer to be able to pen the letter. The purpose for such a statement will be considered later in that section of the letter. Meanwhile the large characters would be very much in evidence.

2. **An unusual style of introduction**. William Barclay tells us of the ancient form of letter writing: "When we read these private letters we find that there was a pattern to which nearly all letters conformed; and we find that the letters of Paul reproduce exactly and precisely the pattern of the letters which people in the ancient world wrote to each other every day."[3] Barclay says this letter form included a greeting, a prayer for their well being, a thanksgiving for the recipients of the letter, the letter's general content, and finally the salutation or personal greetings. But in this introduction, both the prayer and the thanksgiving are omitted. According to Barclay, this omission could not have been missed. Was it an oversight due to the intensity of Paul's personal feelings for the Galatians' fickleness and lack of gospel perception, or was it intentional? Whatever the reason the Galatians would surely feel the sting of the omission.

   This unusual omission also helps us to feel something of the highs and lows of Paul's own emotions as he struggles in the urgency of the moment with a preoccupation on how best to communicate the seriousness and the solution of the Galatians' error to the point of omitting a standardized and expected greeting. When the Holy Spirit guided the writers of Scripture, He did not de-personalize them. He overruled to insure the accuracy of the message divinely intended (cf.1 Corinthians 2:6-13). But the writer's humanness bleeds through.

3. **Paul's unusual disclaimer: a key to interpreting Galatians.** His opening words affirming his apostleship are followed, uniquely, by a disclaimer, *"Paul, an apostle (not sent from men nor through the agency of man, but through Jesus Christ and God the Father)."* Why the disclaimer? None of his other letters following the affirmation of his apostleship contain this defensive qualification. A single reading of Galatians reveals that Paul was defending his apostleship, his gospel (Chs. 1 and 2), and his character (4:16-18; 6:11, 14-17) against charges brought against him by the false teachers at Galatia. We deduce, then, that the false teachers' modus operandi, which was necessary

for them to superimpose their teaching on the apostle's teaching, was to discredit both Paul's person and apostleship. By this means they had effectively overcome the Galatians' strong fraternity for Paul (4:14, 15), as well as his apostolic authority. This explains Paul's disclaimer and why he stressed his divine appointment to the apostleship.

This important key to understanding Paul's particular line of defense becomes a principle for interpreting Galatians: Paul's line of self-defense exposes the false teachers' line of attack.

B. CHRIST TO THE RESCUE: THE GOSPEL ENCAPSULATED

1. **Grace and peace** (1:3). Without exception, every epistle that bears Paul's name is introduced and concluded with a statement of grace to the correspondents. Because of the incredible extravagance of God's love manifested to all men in the unspeakable gift of Christ, this pattern of greeting and salutation cannot be considered a mere formality. It is Paul's genuine intent that all Christians remember and appreciate the totally unearned gift of justification by grace and be strengthened in the resulting peace that is ours forever.

The opposite of grace and peace is the idea of legalistic merit and its resulting anxiety. By the very nature of legalism (trusting in flesh-power for salvation), one can never be certain of his relationship with God. The harder he tries the more peace eludes him.

Grace and peace are words of substance for the Christian. They literally encapsulate the alpha and the omega of the gospel: grace from God and peace for the justified.

2. **Christ came on a rescue mission**.

a. **"who gave Himself *for* our sins"** (1:4). The little word "for" has a big meaning. It is a word of substitution and has been translated "on behalf of." In this phrase, Paul has encapsulated the entire gospel of salvation by grace. Our salvation is grounded in what God Himself has done for us through Christ on the cross. "I have been crucified with Christ; and it is no longer I who live, but Christ lives in me;

and the life which I now live in the flesh I live by faith in the Son of God, who loved me and gave Himself up for me" (2:20). And again, "Christ redeemed us from the curse of the Law, having become a curse for us" (3:13). These statements, when perceptively understood, mitigate legalism.

God did not give us commandments merely to see how well we observe them. He gave Christ as sacrifice on our behalf in order to save us. Thus Isaiah's, "But He was pierced through for our transgressions, He was crushed for our iniquities; The chastening for our well-being fell upon Him, And by His scourging we are healed" (53:5). Peter echoes this remarkable deed: "Christ also suffered for you ...He Himself bore our sins in His body on the cross... for by His wounds you were healed" (1 Peter 2:21-24).

b. **"that He might rescue us from this present evil age"** (1:4). The word *deliver* means "to set free," or "to rescue." The idea of a rescue is to deliver or set free one who could not effect his own deliverance. The human condition in sin is such that man cannot atone for his own sins by the bootstrap method of self-effort in commandment keeping. When Peter on Pentecost exhorted the multitude, "Be saved from this perverse generation," (Acts 2:40) he was encouraging them to respond to God on the grounds of faith in Christ as Lord by repentance and baptism for deliverance from sin. The obedience commanded was to be the expression of faith in Christ to rescue them. The Galatians received from Paul the same message of grace by faith and the same command to accept the Savior's rescue at baptism (Galatians 3:26, 27). At the very moment our faith in Christ leads us to renounce the world for the sovereignty of Christ and be baptized as an expression of faith in Him to save us, our rescue has been divinely achieved. Attempted obedience to the law God gave at Sinai could not achieve deliverance. It could only condemn the sinner. Thus the need for the Galatian letter.

II. The Seriousness of the False Teaching at Galatia, 1:6-10

I am amazed that you are so quickly deserting Him who called you by the grace of Christ, for a different gospel; which is really not another; only there are some who are disturbing you and want to distort the gospel of Christ. But even if we, or an angel from heaven, should preach to you a gospel contrary to what we have preached to you, he is to be accursed! As we have said before, so I say again now, if any man is preaching to you a gospel contrary to what you received, he is to be accursed! For am I now seeking the favor of men, or of God? Or am I striving to please men? If I were still trying to please men, I would not be a bond-servant of Christ (Galatians 1:6-10).

Paul details the seriousness of the Galatian error as (1) a removal from God, (2) a perverted, distorted gospel, (3) resulting in a troubled, disturbed church, (4) a doctrine that will eternally condemn its teachers, and (5) is totally unacceptable to God.

A. IT WAS EQUAL TO DESERTING GOD, 1:6

It is God who calls us through the agency of the gospel (2 Thessalonians 2:14; Acts 2:39). It was not a movement or an idea the Galatians were deserting, but God Himself and the saving grace of Christ. To embrace legalism is to desert God inasmuch as legalism substitutes man in place of God.

For the Galatians then, or for Christians now, to appeal for salvation to a legal system that demands sinless perfection and that condemns the violator at the first infraction is a logical contradiction of the gospel message that God freely offers saving grace by the means of trusting in Christ. Legalism is salvation by faith in self and the exercise of human merit. The gospel message is that, inasmuch as man in fact cannot save himself by such legal means, God can and will save us on the condition that we place our trust and our lives in Christ. But false teachers at Galatia affirmed that grace plus law equaled salvation. Paul replies that, like antipodes that repel, law and gospel by their antipodal natures simply cannot amalgamate. Galatians teaches that if a Christian embraces law as a necessary coordinate of salvation, or if he perverts the works of grace and faith into works of credit and merit, he in reality, by the nature of the case, deserts God, gospel, and grace.

B. IT WAS A PERVERTED GOSPEL, 1:6, 7

1. **Contrasting terms**. Paul uses two words to contrast the irreconcilable difference between legalism and gospel. He speaks of another (*heteros*) gospel, that is, another of a different kind, and says it is not an *allos* gospel, another of the same kind. Legalism is the opposite of the gospel. To call it "gospel" is a misnomer. Paul will not allow this distorted doctrine the name of "gospel."

    The "gospel" with which Paul had to deal at Galatia was a distortion, a perversion, of the gospel of free grace by faith. The Judaizers were saying that Gentile Christians had to keep the law of Moses to continue in a saved state, and that process began with circumcision. But this placed faith in what human flesh could do rather than in what God had done through Christ. These Judaizers were placing faith in the wrong person. The gospel of salvation by faith was thus perverted away from Christ and into a system of self-trust.

2. **Modern gospel perversion**. When sincere and dedicated Christians today express their anxiety that they are not sure they have done enough to be saved, they are exposing a perverted concept of the gospel. They are viewing the law of faith as a legal system, their works of faith as meritorious. Their trust has been perverted inwardly upon themselves that they can do enough Christian deeds to outweigh their sins rather than trust God to continually forgive and cleanse them from every sin while they continually walk, however imperfectly, in the light.

C. TEACHERS OF LEGALISM ARE ACCURSED, 1:8, 9

1. **Anathema, accursed**. The seriousness of the error at Galatia, and in the church today, is exhibited in the NIV translation of Paul's opening words:

    But even if we or an angel from heaven should preach a gospel other than the one we preached to you, let him be eternally condemned (1:8).

    Paul the Christian includes himself in the curse of eternal condemnation that would be pronounced upon those who preach justification by works of law and call it the gospel of Christ. His use of "anathema," eternally condemned, elsewhere defines the sense he intends to communicate, that of being separated from God. "For I could wish that I myself were anathema from Christ for my brethren's sake, my kinsmen according to the flesh" (Romans 9:3, ASV). Even as Christ became a curse for us on the cross (Galatians 3:13), and thereby paid the price of our sin by being separated from God (Isaiah 53:5-8; Matthew 27:46; 2 Corinthians 5:21), so Paul, in his love for his Hebrew brethren who had rejected Christ, wishes he could take the penalty of their unbelief by suffering separation from God for them. Again, he pronounces the curse of separation upon anyone who loves not the Lord: "let him be Anathema" (1 Corinthians 16:22, KJV). The Galatian letter clearly teaches that legalism is a death blow to the Christian's salvation, the theology of the impossibility of apostasy notwithstanding. Those who teach it and those who practice it are eternally accursed from God. Hence the seriousness of the false teaching at Galatia and the urgent need of the Galatian message for them and us.

2. **As we have said before, so I say again now**. The "said before" does not refer back to verse 8, as though Paul is stressing in verse 9 what he said in verse 8. Notice that the words *we* and *I* are used to point out that Paul is now repeating in his letter what he and his companions had said to the Galatians when they were with them in person: "As *we* have said before, so *I* say again now." His point is to impress them with the seriousness of the false teaching at Galatia by reminding them of the warning he gave them when he was in their presence.

   This explains why Paul was "amazed" that they had so quickly deserted the truth. He had warned them that these false teachers were coming, and what they would say. Hardly had he left Galatia before they came, and the Galatians fell prey to their teaching.

D. LEGALISM DOES NOT PLEASE GOD, 1:10

It seems that the Judaizers undermined the Galatians' respect for Paul by accusing him of being a man-pleaser by offering them a watered-down version of the gospel that made no moral requirements. It is, however, rather obvious that if that were the case, Paul would not have been as boldly forthright as he had just been in labeling the Judaizers as perverters of the true gospel, troublemakers, and accursed teachers (1:6-9). While that accusation was not the most tactful way to introduce the subject, Paul knew that such a doctrine perverted both the gospel and the church, and he was of no disposition to keep silent about it. He would please God with both the truth of the gospel and the defense of it even if it did not please the false teachers at Galatia, or those who had bought into their perversion. Such a condemnation at the beginning of a letter is not the way a man-pleaser goes about attempting to win popularity.

CONCLUSION: The truth of the gospel was being distorted by Jewish legalists who attacked Paul's character as self-serving, his apostleship as self-appointed, and his gospel as inadequate. He responds with urgency, affirming his divine appointment to the apostleship, asserting the pernicious error of the Judaizers' doctrine, and pointing to the disturbance among the churches as a natural consequence of the Judaizers' teaching. Such a candid introduction with condemnations of false teaching and false teachers manifested Paul's true character as one who would please God even if it did not please men.

Spiritual Probing
Chapter Two

1. What characteristic differences exist between a book and a letter? How is that significant for the Galatians student?

2. We have stated that Galatians is an unusual correspondence because of three atypical characteristics that would have caught the Galatians' attention upon unscrolling and reading the first statements of the letter. What are those characteristics? What do you think are the implications of each?

3. Paul stated that the false teaching at Galatia was a distorted or perverted gospel. Can you explain the nature of this false teaching in comparison to the truth of the gospel?

4. How serious was this distortion? Could it have affected the eternal salvation of the Galatians? Of Christians today? Are there other statements in the Galatian letter that lead you to your conclusions?

5. We have said that reading Galatians is something like listening to one side of a telephone conversation. One surmises what is being said at the other end by deducing from what one hears at this end. With that as a guideline what do you suppose is behind Paul's three statements in Galatians 1:10?

6. Are we training ourselves to think and to operate on Bible principles like Paul? How shall we respond to brethren who are caught up in a legalism or a liberalism that can claim their souls? Will Galatians 5:2, 4 help? Will God expect us to respond to error in defense of the truth of the gospel as did Paul? According to Galatians 1:6-8, what could be the motivation for such a defensive response?

Chapter Three
From Fanaticism to Faith
Galatians 1:11-24

Paul's Apostleship and Gospel Discredited

Galatians is a defense of the truth of the gospel. Paul had only recently brought the Galatians to justification by faith in Christ. Soon afterwards, however, supposedly Christian Jews convinced the Galatian churches that they had to be circumcised and keep the law of Moses in order to be saved. For these Judaizers to succeed they had to superimpose their teaching onto Paul's apostolic teaching. To accomplish this they had to discredit Paul's apostleship, and consequently his authority, in order to discredit his gospel. And they succeeded, for the Galatians had already begun to observe Jewish ritual (4:8-10), and apparently some had yielded to circumcision (5:2-4). So successful were the Judaizers at Galatia that Paul spent the first one-third of his letter defending and reestablishing his apostolic authority and the integrity of his gospel.

I. The Historical Nature of Paul's Defense

A mere denial of the charges made against him would neither vindicate Paul nor disprove the allegations brought against him. He would have to offer evidence for his defense. To be effective the evidence would have to satisfy an investigation. Paul chose to sustain his claim by relating certain relevant histories from his life and the apostles' lives that were obviously at variance with the charges made against him. His defense had to survive the acid test for the truth of any historical testimony, that of being written at a time when the many persons involved in the evidence were still living to either verify or deny its historical factuality.

A. THE LINE OF DEFENSE REVEALS THE LINE OF ATTACK

Each of the four arguments not only defends Paul and his gospel, but reveals to the reader the line of argumentation the false teachers used against him. The first argument (1:13, 14) reasons that no combination of human efforts could have reached Paul with the gospel in the days of his fanatical persecution of the church. This seeks to confirm his claim that he received the gospel from Christ and not from man. Such defensive reasoning exposes the charge of the false teachers that Paul received his gospel from men and not from the Lord. The second argument (1:15-24) reasons that after conversion he could not have received further gospel instruction from either the apostles at Jerusalem or the churches of Judea. This indicates that the false teachers alleged that Paul received the gospel from one or both of these sources. The third argument (2:1-10) shows Paul's gospel was identical to the apostles' gospel. This reveals that the Judaizers charged his gospel as different from the apostles' gospel. The fourth argument (2:11-21) is a defense of Paul's consistency of doctrine and practice to counter the charge that he was inconsistent. The Judaizers were charging the very opposite of Paul's defensive arguments.

B. THE HISTORICAL CONTEXT OF PAUL'S DEFENSE

Notice the specifics in this autobiographical section demarcating the historical context in which the arguments are couched. Because of this context Paul's claims could be checked out for accuracy.

1. **The time element.** The first event transpired while Paul was yet in Judaism (1:13, 14). The second followed immediately upon his conversion to three years after conversion (1:15-24). The third event took place some seventeen years after conversion (2:1-10), and the fourth happened yet some time later (2:11-21).

2. **Geographical locations**. The events in Paul's evidence occurred in the regions of Arabia, Syria, and Cilicia, and he specifies the cities of Damascus, Jerusalem, and Antioch of Syria.

3. **Persons involved.** In the first argument (1:13, 14) Paul refers to the church as a witness to the fact that he persecuted Christians

up to the time of his conversion. The second argument (1:15-24) focuses on Peter and the Lord's brother James and the churches of Judea. The third argument (2:1-10) spotlights Titus and Barnabas and the apostles at Jerusalem. The final argument (2:11-21) centers upon Peter and Barnabas and certain ones who came from James.

4. **The events themselves are embedded within this historical framework**. What F. F. Bruce said of Luke's writings can be said here of this section of Galatians: "A writer who thus relates his story to the wider context of world history is courting trouble if he is not careful; he affords his critical readers so many opportunities for testing his accuracy."[1]

That the Galatian letter has come down to us today as apostolic, preserved as a part of the New Testament canon, is adequate proof that the persons closest to the events recorded, the Galatians themselves, found Paul's claims for himself and his gospel to be both historically and doctrinally true.

II. The Propositional Statement, 1:11, 12

For I would have you know, brethren, that the gospel which was preached by me is not according to man. For I neither received it from man, nor was I taught it, but I received it through a revelation of Jesus Christ (1:11, 12).

Paul's affirmation of his apostleship at the beginning of his letters is not at all unusual. But his twofold disclaimer that neither his apostolic appointment (1:1) nor his gospel were from men (1:11, 12) is very unusual. It appears that the legalists at Galatia had accused Paul's gospel of being more man-made than divine, that he had received it from man, unlike the original apostles who had received it by divine revelation. Paul wants the Galatians to understand that he, too, received his gospel by direct revelation from Christ. This claim, then, becomes the proposition, the thing to be proved.

A. PAUL'S FOURFOLD CLAIM

The following enlarges the four points of his claim:

1. **Paul's gospel was not according to man**. That is, it was not a man-made teaching. It did not originate from man as the Judaizers alleged.

2. **Paul's gospel was not received from man**. This involves the idea of agency in the transmission of the gospel to Paul. From whom did he receive it? Paul insists there was no human agency in God's transmission of the gospel to him.

3. **Paul was not taught the gospel by a man**. That is, he was not educated to the gospel by the classroom method of teaching.

These last two statements of the claim lead us naturally to focus on the assigned ministry that Christ gave to Ananias in Paul's behalf as recorded in Acts 9:10-19; 22:10-16. Luke tells us that in the days of Paul's persecution of the church, Christ made a special post-resurrection conversion appearance to Paul, stopping him dead in his tracks en route to Damascus, and redirecting him to a certain residence in the city where he would be further instructed. Luke makes it clear that Christ had already instructed Paul in the gospel before Ananias had received his commission from the Lord to go to Paul to restore his sight and baptize him into Christ. Ananias' own statement to Paul of what constituted his commission is clearly defined: "that you may regain your sight, and be filled with the Holy Spirit." Paul's blindness was immediately healed, and he arose and was baptized.

There are no statements in the Acts accounts of Paul's conversion from which it is necessary to deduct that Ananias taught Paul anything of the gospel. All such conclusions would be deducting more from the language than the language itself allows and would furthermore be contrary to Paul's own claim that he neither received the gospel from man, nor had been taught it by the slow classroom process of instruction.

4. **"But" he received it by a direct revelation from Jesus Christ**. Of the words in the original language that are translated "but," this is the strongest. With this last statement, Paul makes a strong contrast between the charge made against him and the actual manner by which he received the gospel.

B. CONSIDER THE WORD *FOR*

There are several words in the original that are translated *for*. This particular word is used to offer the reason something is said or done. Paul uses *for* to introduce each verse in Galatians 1:10-13. He uses it to mean, Let me tell you why, or Let me explain the reason for that statement. First, he makes a claim for the gospel: "the gospel which was preached by me is not according to man." Then in the following statement he offers the reason for the truth of that claim and introduces it with the word *for*: "For I neither received it from man, nor was I taught it. "

After Paul makes his fourfold claim (1:11, 12), he then proceeds to offer in historical sequence four events from his past as proof of the claim (1:13-2:21) and introduces his argumentation with *for*: "For you have heard of my former manner of life..." (1:13).

III. Paul's First Defensive Argument: His Manner of Life in Judaism Before Conversion, 1:13, 14

For you have heard of my former manner of life in Judaism, how I used to persecute the church of God beyond measure, and tried to destroy it; and I was advancing in Judaism beyond many of my contemporaries among my countrymen, being more extremely zealous for my ancestral traditions (Galatians 1:13, 14).

This is a three-pronged argument. It draws from Paul's pre-Christian life in Judaism. The severity of his opposition to Christianity, his advancement in Judaism, and his loyalty to what he believed was true combined to produce a personality that could not be reached with the gospel by any human means. Due to his particular Judaistic mind-set, if Saul were to be converted, it would require a special intervention from heaven. Tenney observed that "the biographical data in Galatians was not written by Paul for the purpose of narrating interesting facts about himself, but as a means of accounting for the stand which he took on the relation of the law and the gospel. He wanted to show to the Galatians that his message...sprang from a divine intervention in his own life."[2]

Paul supports his claim of divine intervention and special instruction from Christ (1:11, 12) with three extraordinary facts from his Judaistic background.

A. SAUL'S FANATICAL PERSECUTION OF THE CHURCH

The extraordinary measure to which Saul of Tarsus persecuted the church gives this part of the argument its force. He does not educate them, but reminds the Galatians that they had already heard of his manner of life prior to his conversion and so expects them to comprehend the full impact of his statement that he persecuted the church "beyond measure."

1. **An historical portrait of Saul the persecutor**. While the ancient Galatians appreciated the implications of that rehearsal we today are dependent on the book of Acts for a historical portrait of Saul the persecutor and the severity to which that persecution extended against the church. Luke's history shows Saul initiating a full-scale persecution of the Jerusalem church by the stoning of Stephen (Acts 7:58—8:1). Christian homes were violated and the occupants dragged off to prison. Not even women were to escape the fury of his wrath (Acts 8:3). He obtained authority from the chief priests to extend his persecutions beyond the borders of Palestine to Damascus, the capital city of Syria (Acts 9:1, 2). There he bound and imprisoned Christians, intending to extradite them to Jerusalem for trial (Acts 9:21). He pursued his persecution with a clear conscience, putting Christians to death on the charge of blasphemy (Acts 26:9-13). His intent was to annihilate Christianity, to make a scorched earth of the church of Christ (Acts 22:4).

2. **An unreachable fanatic**. Prior to conversion, Saul had no remorse nor pangs of conscience for such extreme measures against the church. As he testifies later, "I thought to myself that I had to do many things hostile to the name of Jesus of Nazareth" (Acts 26:9). His persecution was grounded in the conviction that what he was doing was right. The picture that emerges presents no ordinary persecutor, but one of a fanatical sort. His turn of mind and spirit were so over enthusiastic that

no human being could have reached him with the gospel. Herein lies Paul's intended meaning that he persecuted the church "beyond measure." This manifests such a depth of contempt for Christ and the church that any reception of the gospel by a human agency would have been unthinkable and impossible.

This is the point Paul intended to make to the Galatians, that he was so unapproachable by Christians, that he so loathed Christianity, and that the charge of the false teachers that he received the gospel by some human Christian agency was clearly a contradiction of the facts. Who could possibly have approached him? A restatement of Bruce's comment regarding this matter is to the point: who could have "convinced such a man of the out-and-out wrongness of his former course, and led him so decisively to abandon previously cherished beliefs for a movement which he had so vigorously opposed."[3] As observed by R.C. Bell, late professor of Bible at Abilene Christian University, "to support this affirmation of divine instruction and ordination, Paul shows that he could not have learned of Christ either before or after his conversion in an ordinary way. Before, with characteristic energy and zeal, he so persecuted 'beyond measure the church of God' that no Christian could have even thought of trying to win him."[4]

Paul had persecuted the church with such fanaticism that the charge of the false teachers that he was taught the gospel by a man was clearly a contradiction of the facts in the case. The strength of the argument was sufficient to convince the Galatians that Paul's claim to have received the gospel from Christ was true.

B. SAUL'S PROMINENCE IN JUDAISM

The word *advance* or *increase* is used by Luke of Jesus who "kept increasing in wisdom and stature, and in favor with God and men" (Luke 2:52). "Josephus describes how as a boy he 'made great progress in education'... this is a common Hellenistic use of the word."[5]

Saul had a very prominent, influential standing among the Jews. He was out front of all his contemporaries scholastically and socially, and he had gained powerful influence among the hierarchy (cf. Acts 9:1, 2; 26:12). He advanced as a scholar at the feet of Gamaliel, the greatest rabbi of his day and leader of the Pharisees (Acts 22:3). From his youth he advanced socially among the Jewish elite as an outstanding Pharisee (Philippians 3:5). His power was manifested in his persecution of the church. He had to have access to funds that would have been essential to the support of such a police action. Such acquisitions raised young, brilliant Saul of Tarsus to a place of prominence in Judaism. Such a prominent fanatic would have been unreachable by any human effort. Paul's point was to demonstrate to the Galatians just how contrary to truth the claim was that he had received his gospel from a man.

C. SAUL'S PHARISAIC LEGALISM

Saul was very zealous for the ancestral traditions of the Pharisees, his Judaic "fathers." His zeal has been portrayed in his fanatical persecution of the church. In this part of the argument Paul explains what it was for which he was so zealous. The "traditions" in Jewish theology were supposedly the oral traditions of the elders from the time of Moses. This oral law was enshrined by the Pharisees and handed down through their schools. These traditions were held to be equal in authority to Scripture. Saul's theology was shaped and crystallized by these traditions from his youth in the school of the Pharisees (Acts 23:6; 26:4, 5). The utter legalism of these traditions by the time of Christ led the Pharisees to reject Jesus as Messiah and prejudiced Saul against the truth of the gospel. As Saul of Tarsus he positioned himself against Christianity from the vantage point of a theological prejudice.

This threefold portrait of Saul's manner of life in Judaism was to convince the Galatians that such a theologically prejudiced, prominent fanatic could not have been reached with the gospel by mere human effort as claimed by the false teachers. His conversion, and therefore his gospel knowledge, could only have come through a supernatural intervention by Christ. Here is a major part of the evidence that convinced the Galatians that Paul's claim to have received the gospel by direct revelation from Christ, and not from any man, was true.

IV. Paul's Second Defensive Argument: He Had No Contact With Human Teachers in the Gospel for Three Years Following Conversion, 1:15-24.

But when He who had set me apart, even from my mother's womb, and called me through His grace, was pleased to reveal His Son in me, that I might preach Him among the Gentiles, I did not immediately consult with flesh and blood, nor did I go up to Jerusalem to those who were apostles before me; but I went away to Arabia, and returned once more to Damascus. Then three years later I went up to Jerusalem to become acquainted with Cephas, and stayed with him fifteen days. But I did not see any other of the apostles except James, the Lord's brother. (Now in what I am writing to you, I assure you before God that I am not lying.) Then I went into the regions of Syria and Cilicia. And I was still unknown by sight to the churches of Judea which were in Christ; but only, they kept hearing, "He who once persecuted us is now preaching the faith which he once tried to destroy." And they were glorifying God because of me (Galatians 1:15-24).

This is a two-pronged argument relating Paul's preaching activities from the time immediately following his conversion at Damascus to three years later. His argumentation is historically constructed to prove to the Galatians that the gospel he preached for three years after conversion could not have been received from either the apostles or the churches of Judea. Apparently the Judaizers had charged that after conversion Paul had been further taught by these sources. To sustain his claim he offers the following evidence.

A. HE HAD NO CONTACT WITH THE ORIGINAL APOSTLES, 1:15-20

Paul's historical reconstruction of his ministry from conversion to three years later found him immediately preaching the gospel from Damascus (cf. Acts 9:19-22) to Arabia and back again to Damascus. His point is that for three years following his conversion he did not journey to Jerusalem. It was only after this three-year preaching stint that he first saw any one of the apostles (Peter), with whom he visited for a short period of fifteen days. Obviously, then, the apostles could not have been his instructors in the gospel. His emphasis on his independence of the apostles stresses that the accuracy of his gospel is due to the Lord's own revelation of the gospel to Paul.

B. HE HAD NO CONTACT WITH THE CHURCHES OF JUDEA, 1:21-24

Notice Paul's use of *then* in Galatians 1:18, 21, and 2:1 to indicate the time that he changed from one locale to another. Paul's "Then I went into the regions of Syria and Cilicia" explains that after his fifteen days with Peter in Judea he did not make contact with the Judean churches, but left for Syria and Cilicia (the latter wherein was Tarsus, Paul's hometown). The Galatians could check this out with Peter if they wished. But Paul offers a further proof that up to that time he was "still unknown by sight to the churches of Judea" (1:22). So neither could they have been a source of Paul's further instruction in the gospel.

This line of reasoning reveals that the Judaizers claimed that Paul was further educated in the gospel after conversion by the apostles, and/or the churches of Judea, rather than having a full revelation of the gospel from Christ as the original apostles had received. But as he had been preaching for three years before meeting with any of the apostles, and inasmuch as the Judean churches during that time could not even identify Paul by sight, it is clear that he did not receive any gospel instruction from them. It is reasonable to believe that Paul received his gospel from Christ even as he claimed.

CONCLUSION: The preceding biographical data, couched in the historical context for verification, is offered by Paul as proof that his claim to have received his gospel by a direct revelation from Jesus Christ is true. This data should expose the erroneous charges of the Judaizers that Paul's knowledge of the gospel came from one or more human agencies and should begin to gain back the confidence of the Galatians that Paul was indeed a divinely appointed apostle.

Spiritual Probing
Chapter Three

1. How were the false teachers at Galatia able to superimpose their erroneous teaching on Paul's apostolic teaching? What was their strategy? Was it effective? How do you know? Can a similar thing happen today in order to superimpose a false teaching on the Bible? Can you give a couple of examples?

2. We have spoken of the historical nature of Paul's defense of his apostleship and gospel. Explain what is meant by the historical context and how Paul's defense is immersed in it.

3. What is meant by saying that the line of defense exposes the line of attack? Can you illustrate this from Galatians?

4. From Paul's disclaimer in Galatians 1:1 and from his fourfold claim in Galatians 1:11, 12, what accusations can we confidently infer the false teachers were making against Paul?

5. Paul makes an argument in Galatians 1:11, 12 as evidence that he did not receive his gospel from a man. Can you present the reasoning of that argument? Can you reason the logistics of his argument in Galatians 1:15-24 that he offered as proof that he did not receive his gospel from a man?

6. Are we aware that, even today, Christians must defend their loyalty to Christ?

Chapter Four
Paul Endorsed
By the Original Apostles
Galatians 2:1-10

Introduction

In this lesson Paul defends his gospel against the charge that it was different from the apostles' gospel. Keep in mind Paul's claim in Galatians 1:11, 12 that he received his gospel by revelation from the Lord and not from man. This section of the letter is the third in a sequence of four historical events that Paul details in defense of that claim.

Then after an interval of fourteen years I went up again to Jerusalem with Barnabas, taking Titus along also. And it was because of a revelation that I went up; and I submitted to them the gospel which I preach among the Gentiles, but I did so in private to those who were of reputation, for fear that I might be running, or had run, in vain. But not even Titus who was with me, though he was a Greek, was compelled to be circumcised. But it was because of the false brethren who had sneaked in to spy out our liberty which we have in Christ Jesus, in order to bring us into bondage. But we did not yield in subjection to them for even an hour, so that the truth of the gospel might remain with you. But from those who were of high reputation (what they were makes no difference to me; God shows no partiality) - well, those who were of reputation contributed nothing to me. But on the contrary, seeing that I had been entrusted with the gospel to the uncircumcised, just as Peter had been to the circumcised (for He who effectually worked for Peter in his apostleship to the circumcised effectually worked for me also to the Gentiles), and recognizing the grace that had been given to me, James and Cephas and John, who were reputed to be pillars, gave to me and Barnabas the right hand of fellowship, that we might go the Gentiles, and they to the circumcised. They only asked us to remember the poor - the very thing I also was eager to do (Galatians 2:1-10).

I. Historical Parallels Between the Jerusalem Meeting of Galatians 2:1-10 and the Jerusalem Conference of Acts 15:1-29

The majority of American and British scholarship has long held the view that Galatians 2:1-10 and Acts 15:1-29 are accounts of the same event at Jerusalem, the so-called Jerusalem Conference, but from different vantage points. Recent studies reveal, however, that some are equating Galatians 2:1-10 with Acts 11:27-30, the Famine Visit. While the resolution to this friendly debate is not essential to an understanding of Galatians 2:1-10, there are several historical parallels between Galatians 2 and Acts 15 that are identical in nature. These parallels offer to us more information regarding the problem and the solution to legalism that existed in the Galatian churches then and also in the churches of Christ today.

A. IDENTIFYING GALATIANS 2:1-10 WITH ACTS 15:1-29

Paul's first missionary journey (Acts 13 and 14) takes him and Barnabas to the Roman province of Galatia where God "opened a door of faith to the Gentiles" (Acts 14:27). A while later "some men came down from Judea and began teaching the brethren, 'Unless you are circumcised according to the custom of Moses, you cannot be saved'" (Acts 15:1). Since the issue, though debated between Paul and Barnabas and Judaizers from Judea, was not resolved, the upshot was the so-called Jerusalem Conference (Acts15:2). There Paul and Barnabas, together with the original apostles and the elders and brethren of the Jerusalem church, discussed the correctness of the position of certain Pharisees who required Gentile Christians to keep the law of Moses. The conclusion, reached by guidance of the Holy Spirit, was that Gentile Christians were free from such legal requirements, that indeed Jews as well as Gentiles were saved by grace through faith in Christ and totally apart from the law of Moses (Acts 15:3-29).

Significantly, Paul's account in Galatians 2:1-10 of his divine assignment to go to Jerusalem fits quite snugly, both chronologically and historically, into Luke's account of the Jerusalem Conference.

Both Galatians 2 and Acts 15 detail the account of the apostles' stand against the law binders, leaving the distinct impression that they are accounts of the same historical events.

B. PARALLELS BETWEEN GALATIANS 2:1-10 AND ACTS 15:1-29

The following comparisons reveal a remarkable sameness of content between the two accounts:

1. The same question about Paul's apostolic authority (Acts 15:1, 2 and Galatians 2:2).

2. The same reason for Paul and Barnabas meeting with the Jerusalem apostles (Acts 15:2 and Galatians 2:2).

3. The same problems: legalism, the binding of circumcision and the law of Moses on Gentile Christians (Acts 15:1, 5 and Galatians 2:3-5).

4. The same persons involved: Paul and Barnabas, Peter and James, false brethren, and Gentile Christians.

5. The same endorsement of Paul and Barnabas (Acts 15:22-27 and Galatians 2:7-9).

C. SOME CONSIDERATIONS REGARDING THE VIEW THAT GALATIANS 2:1-10 IS HISTORICALLY PARALLEL WITH ACTS 11:27-30

1. **Why the reenactment of a done deal**? Keep in mind the historical parallels between Galatians 2:1-10 and Acts 15:1-29. If Galatians 2 is actually paralleled by Acts 11:27-30, then the same people are going to reenact the same roles, re-debate the same subject, and the Holy Spirit will re-guide them to reach the same conclusion all over again in Acts 15! This would require that the Holy Spirit would have to re-guide the same apostles to reach the same conclusion in Acts 15 that He had already led them to conclude in Acts 11. Echo answers, why?

2. **Why did Paul go to Jerusalem in Acts 11:27-30?** Is the reason for Paul's visit to Jerusalem in Acts 11:27-30 commensurate with the reason he gives in Galatians 2:2? It is stated in Acts 11:27-30 that Paul's purpose for going to Jerusalem at that time was to carry needed funds to the Jewish brethren for famine relief. But the reason Paul gives for his journey to Jerusalem in Galatians 2:2 is to

confirm his gospel and to defend it against legalism. And this is also the same reason Luke gives in Acts 15 for Paul's journey to Jerusalem. The reasons for Paul's two Jerusalem visits in Acts 11 and Acts 15 are quite different. Acts 15 is the only statement of purpose that corresponds to the one given in Galatians 2:2.

3. **An anachronism to be considered**. Paul was converted not earlier than one year after Christ's crucifixion, approximately 31 A.D. According to the reckoning of three years from Paul's conversion to his initial meeting with Peter (Galatians 1:15-18), and then another fourteen years from that time until Paul was assigned to go to Jerusalem (Galatians 2:1) is a total of seventeen years from conversion to the date of the Jerusalem Conference at about 48 A.D., the date generally accepted.

31 AD. Paul's conversion.

+<u>17</u> years later Paul goes to Jerusalem (Galatians 2:1).

48 AD date of Jerusalem Conference (Acts 15; Galatians 2).

However, if the view that Galatians 2:1-10 is historically commensurate with Acts 11:27-30, a serious anachronism seems to emerge from these considerations that contradicts this view. Paul's famine visit in Acts 11 occurred about the time of Herod Agrippa's death (Acts 12:1-25), which was 44 A.D. But according to Galatians 2:1, that famine visit was seventeen years after Paul's conversion. That means Paul had to be converted seventeen years before 44 AD., which would be about 27 AD., during the ministry of Christ - an unacceptable conversion date.

44 A.D. Herod's death, Paul's famine visit to Jerusalem Acts 11.

-<u>17</u> years earlier Paul converted.

27 A.D. Placing Paul's conversion during Christ's ministry.

It appears that the Jerusalem visit of Acts 11:27-30 is too early to be the Jerusalem visit of Galatians 2. Even in consideration of the Jewish system of reckoning time, subtracting a year or two from the seventeen years of Galatians 2:2 does not appear to resolve an apparent anachronism.

II. Paul's Third Defensive Argument: Endorsed By the Apostles, 2:1-10

Keep in mind that the line of defense reveals the line of attack. This defense reveals that the false teachers at Galatia attacked Paul's gospel charging it was not the same as the apostles' gospel. Paul had to defend his gospel against that charge.

A. GOD DIRECTS PAUL TO JERUSALEM FOR A CONFIRMATION OF HIS GOSPEL BY THE ORIGINAL APOSTLES, 2:1, 2

1. **Consider the use of *then* as a time indicator.** Paul writes, "Then after an interval of fourteen years I went up again to Jerusalem" (Galatians 2:1). Sometimes the impression is left that Paul is a bit ambiguous regarding the time interval of years from his conversion to this divinely assigned journey to Jerusalem. It is urged by some that we cannot be certain that this fourteen years is reckoned from his visit with Peter three years after conversion (Galatians 1:18), making a total of seventeen years from conversion to this particular Jerusalem visit, or whether this fourteen-year interval is the total number of years from conversion.

    However, Paul uses the word *then* three times in Galatians 1:15-2:1 to indicate a chronological sequence of events that begins from the time of his conversion. After recounting his conversion in Damascus, his preaching circuit into Arabia, and his return to Damascus (Galatians 1:15-17), he writes, "*Then* three years later I went up to Jerusalem to become acquainted with Cephas" (Galatians 1:18). Clearly, it was three years from conversion to this visit with Peter. After this visit he states, "*Then* I went into the regions of Syria and Cilicia" (Galatians 1:21). This "then" easily follows the visit with Cephas. Finally he writes, "*Then* after an interval of fourteen years," that is, following his last journey into Syria and Cilicia, he "went up again to Jerusalem." The language is intentionally punctuated with his "then" statements clearly pointing out the time intervals from conversion to his meeting with Peter three years later, *then* on to Syria and Cilicia, and *then* to Jerusalem yet fourteen years later. The clarity of the language belies the charge of ambiguity. It was seventeen years plus (if we add the unstated amount of time it required for Paul to go to Syria and Cilicia) to this important visit to Jerusalem *again*.

This "again" does not indicate that this was Paul's second visit to Jerusalem. Any number of visits to Jerusalem could have transpired between his visit with Peter three years after conversion and this particular Jerusalem visit fourteen years later. But in context of Galatians 1:18-2:1, Paul is clarifying that from the time he went to Jerusalem to visit Peter until he went up to Jerusalem "again" for this special meeting there was a fourteen-year interval.

2. **Paul went to Jerusalem by revelation**. Paul's underlying reason for going to Jerusalem this time was due to a direct assignment from the Lord (Galatians 2:2). But Acts 15:2 says that after Paul and Barnabas debated the Judaizers about Christian freedom from the law that "the brethren determined" that they should go to Jerusalem about the matter. This variation as to who sent Paul to Jerusalem presents no contradiction between Luke's account in Acts and Paul's in Galatians. It is a matter of vantage points, one divine and the other human. We find a similar wording in Acts 13:1-4. Here the Holy Spirit through the prophets at Antioch (of Syria) instructed the church to choose Paul and Barnabas for a special evangelistic assignment. Then Luke writes in the next sentence that the brethren "sent them away." Thus the Holy Spirit was the initiator of the mission and the brethren obediently sent them away. Both the divine and the human are involved in the sending. Similarly Paul says in Galatians 2:1 that "it was because of a revelation that I went up," and Luke writes in Acts 15:2 that "the brethren determined that Paul and Barnabas and certain others of them [like Titus] should go up to Jerusalem." Both the divine and the human are included in the matter of sending Paul to Jerusalem.

3. **Paul submits his gospel to the apostles in private**, "for fear that I might be running, or had run, in vain," (Galatians 2:2).

There is no indication here that Paul doubts either himself or his gospel. He defends his message as "the truth of the gospel" (cf. Galatians 2:5, 14). But at this time both his gospel and his apostleship seem to be under suspicion, probably due to the Judaizers' allegations. Therefore, in agreement with the Lord's wisdom, Paul submits his gospel to the original apostles for their investigation and authoritative endorsement as a preventative measure against the discrediting of any of his former work and the future of his missionary evangelism.

B. PAUL'S FOUR-PRONGED ARGUMENT IN DEFENSE OF HIS GOSPEL, 2:1-10

The student should keep before him Paul's purpose for relating the events of the Jerusalem meeting of Acts 15 to the Galatians. It is that they might identify the Judaistic teaching in their own midst as the same teaching that the apostles and elders at Jerusalem opposed.

1. **Titus was not compelled to be circumcised**. Verses 1 and 2 state that Barnabas and Titus accompanied Paul on the spcial assignment to Jerusalem. As an uncircumcised Greek, Titus, a Christian brother, was an ideal "test case" regarding the validity of Paul's gospel. Since the apostles did not compel Titus to be circumcised it was a "case closed" kind of evidence that the law was not binding on Gentile Christians, as the false teachers at Galatia affirmed, and that Paul's gospel of justification by faith in Christ was indeed apostolic. It was an exposé of the error of legalism at Galatia.

2. **The apostles were united in their stand against the false teachers**. It is rather conclusive from the total content of this entire section that those of "high reputation" had already endorsed Paul and Bamabas with "the right hand of fellowship" prior to their united public defense against the false teachers at Jerusalem. Having earlier evaluated Paul's gospel "in private," and concluding that he had "been entrusted with the gospel" by the same One "who effectually worked for Peter," they were now ready to publicly face the false brethren in a united, unyielding stand for "the truth of the gospel." Hence Paul's, "But

we did not yield in subjection to them for even an hour, so that the truth of the gospel might remain with you." The *we* embraces all the apostles that were present and all the brethren at Jerusalem who were united by a common gospel.

3. **The apostles added nothing to Paul's gospel.** When Paul arrived at Jerusalem he went into private session with the apostles and submitted his gospel before them for their investigation. They discovered that they could add nothing to it, but perceived that Paul had been "entrusted with the gospel" by the same Lord who worked His grace through Peter. Since there was nothing of gospel knowledge that they could impart to Paul it would be further proof to the Galatians that his gospel was the same as the apostles' gospel. It would also seem that poetic justice was dealt to the Judaizers, for now their gospel had been exposed as contrary to the apostles' gospel.

4. **The apostles endorsed Paul and Bamabas.** When the apostles "recogniz[ed] the grace that had been given" to Paul they extended to him and Barnabas "the right hand of fellowship." This "right hand of fellowship" was clearly an endorsement that Paul's gospel was the same as the gospel preached by Peter, James and John, and gave the lie to those of the circumcision that Paul's gospel was not apostolically authoritative.

    CONCLUSION: The message to the Galatians would be clear. Such an endorsement from those of high reputation and authority in the church vindicated Paul's gospel and his years of preaching the sufficiency of justification by faith in Christ apart from the law of Moses. It would reaffirm the Galatians' original confidence in Paul and deliver a crushing blow to the legalists and their doctrine of salvation by legal works.

Spiritual Probing
Chapter Four

1. Many students of the Galatian letter believe that Paul's account of the Jerusalem meeting in Galatians 2:1-10 corresponds historically with the account of the so-called Jerusalem Conference of Acts 15:1-21. Present the historical parallels between these two meetings in evidence for this persuasion.

2. Others believe the account of Galatians 2:1-10 is historically parallel with Acts 11:27-30. Present evidence for this belief. Can you present some of the considerations in this chapter that are reasons for not believing this view? What are your personal thoughts on the matter? Will either view add or subtract from Paul's message to the Galatians?

3. We have observed that Paul makes a four-pronged argument in Galatians 2:1-10 that his gospel is the same as the gospel of the original apostles. Since the line of defense exposes the line of attack, what can we infer was the reason for this particular defense? Can you restate those four historical events in Paul's argument? Can you present Paul's intended reasoning from the facts to the conclusion?

4. From the statements in Galatians 2:2, 7, 9 what view of Paul can we infer the original apostles might have had of him at this time? Who or what do you suppose caused the apostles to think that way? What, then, could we infer was the apostles' reason for having Paul present his gospel to them in closed session? Paul says he went to Jerusalem by a direct revelation from God (Galatians 2:1, 2). From our study of the Judaizers' accusations against Paul's gospel, what do you think God's intention was for this session with the apostles?

5. Why do we say that Titus was a "test case" in Paul's reasoning? What was actually being tested? How would this test prove Paul's gospel to be apostolic?

6. Do you recognize from this lesson that it may sometimes be necessary for one Christian to come to the aid of another when he is unjustly criticized for teaching a Bible doctrine?

An Apostolic Rebuke
Galatians 2:11-21

In this lesson Paul makes a fourth and final defense for his claim that he received his gospel from Christ and not from man. Remember that Paul's line of defense exposes the line of attack the false teachers used to discredit him and his gospel. This part of the letter appears to disclose an attempt by them to have modeled Peter as an example of law keeping to contrast with Paul who taught its non-essentiality.

However, Paul shows that Peter knew that the law was not still binding and that he lived out its implications upon the law by eating with the Gentile Christians at Antioch of Syria. Then Paul points to a serious inconsistency by Peter. Assuming that he would be labeled a minister of sin by some visiting Jews, Peter withdrew from the Gentile brethren, intentionally leaving the impression that the law was yet binding and that Gentile Christians without the law were yet sinners. Paul seizes on this incident and explains to the Galatians the implications of this hypocrisy upon Peter's conduct, upon Christ's integrity, and upon God's grace.

Paul's ultimate reason for relating this incident was to expose the same erroneous implications upon the legalistic teaching at Galatia, and to defend the truth of the gospel as he originally taught it.

This section of Galatians comes in two parts: the historical occasion (2:11-13), and Paul's public rebuke of Peter (2:14-21).

I. The Occasion: Peter's Conduct at Antioch, 2:11-13

But when Cephas came to Antioch, I opposed him to his face, because he stood condemned. For prior to the coming of certain men from James, he used to eat with the Gentiles; but when they came, he began to withdraw and hold himself aloof, fearing the party of the circumcision. And the rest of the Jews joined him in hypocrisy, with the result that even Barnabas was carried away with their hypocrisy (Galatians 2:11-13).

Historically, this incident follows the Jerusalem meeting just related in Galatians 2:1-10 where Peter stood with Paul against the legalism at Jerusalem. This is clearly indicated by the language, "But when Cephas came to Antioch...." The introductory word *But* sets up a contrast between Peter's teaching at Jerusalem and the inconsistency of his conduct at Antioch.

A. INITIALLY PETER ATE WITH THE GENTILES, 2:12

Every Jew knew the Mosaic regulations regarding clean and unclean meats (Leviticus 11). But with the abolition of the law of Moses those restrictions fell. Peter knew that and understood its implications upon the food regulations of the law. Characteristic of his eager nature, he plunged into table fellowship with the Gentile brethren at Antioch. Such conduct was tantamount to an apostolic statement that the law of Moses was no longer binding.

This was not Peter's first experience at fellowship with Gentile converts in Christianity. He had already come to understand through his conversion of Cornelius that the Lord makes no distinction between Jews and Gentiles. Luke writes,

Peter went up on the housetop about the sixth hour to pray. And he became hungry, and was desiring to eat; but while they were making preparations, he fell into a trance; and he beheld the sky opened up, and a certain object like a great sheet coming down, lowered by four corners to the ground, and there were in it all kinds of four-footed animals and crawling creatures of the earth and birds of the air. And a voice came to him, "Arise, Peter, kill and eat!" But Peter said, "By no means, Lord, for I have never eaten anything unholy and unclean." And again a voice came to him a second time, "What God has cleansed, no longer consider unholy." And this happened three times (Acts 10:9-16).

Though at the moment Peter was "greatly perplexed," the Lord explained the meaning of the vision by directing him to preach the gospel to the household of the Roman centurion Cornelius. Since Christianity began at Pentecost, the gospel had not been preached to uncircumcised non-law keeping Gentiles as they had not been considered by Jewish Christians worthy of hearing the gospel. But through this Spirit-led experience Peter saw that the gospel was for all men. The implication of Peter's housetop vision and conversion of Cornelius regarding the law of Moses was that it was no longer binding. Peter explained this to the brethren at Jerusalem (Acts 11:1-18). Later, at the Jerusalem conference (Acts 15), it was Peter who championed the Gentiles' freedom from the law of Moses. Therefore, when Peter ate with the Gentiles at Antioch it was a nonverbal statement from an apostle that the law was no longer binding and that the dietary food restrictions had passed away with it.

B. LATER PETER PRETENDED THE LAW WAS STILL BINDING, 2:12,13

Peter's initial course of action with the predominately Gentile church at Antioch was dictated by Christian love. He ate with his Gentile brethren. But "his heart carried him farther than his later judgment was prepared to go."[1] For when certain Christian Jews came from James, Peter sensed in them a Jewish predisposition toward Gentiles akin to that which he had experienced at Jerusalem when returning from the conversion of Cornelius (Acts 11:1-3). Peter was quickly caught up in the crosscurrents of peer pressure and traditional Hebrew acculturation. Overawed by men, Peter played the hypocrite (from *hypokirsis*, meaning to "answer from under" and was commonly used of an actor playing a part and pretending to be what he was not). He drew back, separating himself from the Gentile brethren, leaving the dual impression that they were sinners outside the law of Moses, and that the law was itself essential to salvation. By this conduct he betrayed his own integrity and inspired insight that "God is not one to show partiality" (Acts 10:34).

Sadly, the current was so strong that it swept up the rest of the Jews, "even Barnabas." If such a wonderful, mature, and insightful man as good Barnabas was not exempt from the temptation to dissimulate, how much more should the rest of us take heed to our heart motives.

II. Paul Rebukes Peter Publicly, 2:14

This section of the Galatian letter is Paul's climactic defense for his apostolic independence from the original apostles and for the truth of his gospel as he originally taught it to the Galatians. In this particular bit of history, Paul may also be defending himself against a Judaistic charge that he was inconsistent in doctrine and practice. After all, had he not circumcised Timothy immediately following the Jerusalem Conference (Acts 16:1-3)? Could that not be twisted into a charge that he taught one thing and practiced another? Thus Paul's purpose for relating this incident may include a defense of his consistency of life and teaching.

A. THE ENTIRE SECTION SEEMS TO CONSTITUTE PAUL'S ADDRESS TO PETER

Some translations indicate, by confining the quotation marks to Galatians 2:14, that Paul's rebuke of Peter begins and ends with that verse. This would likewise indicate the rest of this section through verse 21 is Paul's instruction to the Galatians rather than the record of his rebuke of Peter. But the NASV seems to be the better interpretation by ending the quotation at verse 21.

1. **Consider Paul's "we...even we...we ourselves" in 2:15-17.** We know Paul is addressing Peter in verse 14. In verse 15 he continues: "We are Jews by nature and not sinners from among the Gentiles." The Galatian churches were without question predominantly Gentile, and Paul and Peter were Jews by nature. Therefore Paul's "we" who "are Jews by nature" (or, "by birth," NIV), cannot be said of these Gentile Galatians. Paul, then, in verses 15-16 is relating to the Galatians what he said to Peter.

    Consider the statement in verse 16: "nevertheless knowing that a man is not justified by the works of the Law." If the Galatians knew that they were not justified by the law, Paul would not have had occasion to write the letter. Of course, Peter being Spirit-led knew that men are justified by faith and not by law, so it seems conclusive that Paul is still addressing Peter about what both of them knew regarding justification. Paul's starting point, then, for his doctrinal argument is an appeal to a mutual basic conviction between himself and Peter.

The "even we" of verse 16 knew that they were not justified by the works of the law, for Paul writes, "nevertheless knowing that a man is not justified by the works of the Law but through faith in Christ Jesus, even we have believed in Christ Jesus." While the apostles knew they were justified by faith in Christ and not by the works of the law, the Galatians were not sure. They had once believed it, having been taught it by Paul. But now false teaching made them doubt. Consequently the "even we" who knew they were justified by faith in Christ refers to Paul and Peter, not to the Galatians who doubted it. It seems conclusive that Paul is yet addressing Peter.

Finally, the "we ourselves" of verse 17 are surely Paul and Peter who had to renounce faith in the law in order to be justified by faith in Christ, and were thereby "found sinners" by the law binders. The indictment that Peter would therefore be found a minister of sin by those who came from James seems to be the base of his fearful reaction in withdrawing from the Gentile brethren. But Paul reasons with Peter that such nonverbal action actually implies that Christ would be the real minister of sin, since it was He who abolished the law and gave Peter His message. This points to Peter as the one to whom these words were addressed.

2. **The "you...we...I" transfer from Peter to Paul**. In verse 14, Paul pointedly singles out Peter for the needed censure by using the personal pronoun "you." In verses 15-17, by using the plural personal pronoun "we...even we...we ourselves," he encourages Peter to stand boldly with him as men who know they are justified by faith in Christ and not by works of the law, who are not willing by their conduct or their teaching to allow the implication that Christ is a minister of sin, though they themselves are by that means found to be sinners. By making a transition to the personal pronoun "I" in verses 18-21, Paul insightfully illustrates for Peter's benefit what inconsistencies are implied, even by a feigned return to the law, against innocent Gentile brethren, against the purpose of God's law, against the power

of faith in Christ to live for God, and against the need for saving grace and the cross of Christ. By transference of "you" to "I" Paul himself assumes the consequences of Peter's implied theology, thus removing from Peter some of the pressure of the moment in a gracious effort to encourage his recovery.

The indication is that Galatians 2:14-21 is a concise statement of Paul's rebuke of Peter at Antioch.

B. PETER SINGLED OUT FOR PUBLIC REBUKE, 2:14

But when I saw that they were not straightforward about the truth of the gospel, I said to Cephas in the presence of all, "If you, being a Jew, live like the Gentiles and not like the Jews, how is it that you compel the Gentiles to live like Jews?" (Galatians 2:14).

1. **Peter's apostolic actions carried much authority with the church**. If his dissimulation were allowed to go unchallenged this incident could take on the appearance of an apostolic precedent. Consequently Peter was singled out for public censure.

2. **Peter's walk was challenged, not his talk**. Another rendering is, "But when I saw that they walked not uprightly according to the truth of the gospel...." (ASV), Paul immediately perceived the contradiction between the gospel for all men without distinction and the discrimination of these Jews against the Gentile brethren at Antioch. When the apostles spoke for God they spoke by the special guidance of the Holy Spirit. Their word selection was overruled by the Spirit, thus insuring the accuracy of the transmission of God's message (1 Corinthians 2:10-13; 2 Peter 1:21). What the apostles "received" by revelation from the Spirit they "delivered" by inspiration from the same Spirit (1 Corinthians 11:23; 15:3). But while God made special provision to guard the apostles' message from error, no such provision was made for their Christian lifestyle. Peter taught the truth of the gospel, and the rest of the Jews knew the truth. But their conduct, their "walk" in this particular instance at Antioch, was a contradiction of the gospel they knew.

   None of the apostles were superhuman beings. They had to fight sin and self as other Christians. Paul indicated as much when he said he had to work at subjecting himself to Christ lest he be disqualified after preaching to others (1 Corinthians 9:27). Their message was divinely preserved from error, but not their lives.

III. Peter's Inconsistencies, 2:14-21

Paul makes it clear that Peter's conduct constitutes an attack on the truth of the gospel:

But when I saw that they were not straightforward about the truth of the gospel, I said to Cephas in the presence of all, "If you, being a Jew, live like the Gentiles and not like the Jews, how is it that you compel the Gentiles to live like Jews? We are Jews by nature, and not sinners from among the Gentiles; nevertheless knowing that a man is not justified by the works of the Law but through faith in Christ Jesus, even we have believed in Christ Jesus, that we may be justified by faith in Christ, and not by the works of the Law; since by the works of the Law shall no flesh be justified. But if, while seeking to be justified in Christ, we ourselves have also been found sinners, is Christ then a minister of sin? May it never be! For if I rebuild what I have once destroyed, I prove myself to be a transgressor. For through the Law I died to the Law, that I might live to God. I have been crucified with Christ; and it is no longer I who live, but Christ lives in me; and the life which I now live in the flesh I live by faith in the Son of God, who loved me, and delivered Himself up for me. I do not nullify the grace of God; for if righteousness comes through the Law, then Christ died needlessly" (Galatians 2:14-21).

There are at least six points of gospel doctrine that Peter repudiates by separating from the Gentile brethren: the unity of the body of Christ (2:14), justification by faith in Christ (2:15, 16), the ministry of Christ that culminated in the cross and removal of the law (2:17), the purpose of the law to convict men of sin (2:19), faith in Christ as the the source of power to live for God (2:20), and the grace of God expressed in the cross of Christ as the ground of our justification (2:21).

Perhaps the word inconsistency best describes Paul's perception of the implications of Peter's conduct. It was inconsistent with the following:

A. PETER'S HYPOCRITICAL CONDUCT AT ANTIOCH WAS IN-CONSISTENT WITH HIS DEFENSE AT JERUSALEM FOR GEN-TILE FREEDOM FROM THE LAW (Galatians 2:3-5; Acts 15:7-11).

Paul had just stated that those at Jerusalem - Peter, John, and James - had not "compelled" the Gentile Titus to be circumcised (Galatians 2:3). But now, after having table fellowship with the Gentile brethren, Peter separates himself from them and by implication would "compel" the Gentiles to be circumcised (Galatians 2:14) - a clearly implied reversal of his doctrinal position. Such discrimination would drive a wedge into the unity of the body of Christ.

B. PETER'S CONDUCT IN SEPARATING HIMSELF FROM THE GENTILE BRETHREN WAS INCONSISTENT WITH HIS EARLIER CONDUCT WHEN HE ENDORSED THEM BY EATING WITH THEM. By this nonverbal action, he was now compelling them to come under the Jewish law which he himself had just implied by eating with them was no longer binding. Such inconsistency, motivated by fear rather than conviction, constituted hypocrisy.

C. PETER'S CONDUCT WAS INCONSISTENT WITH WHAT HE AS AN INSPIRED APOSTLE KNEW VERY WELL TO BE TRUE, THAT WE ARE JUSTIFIED BY FAITH IN CHRIST AND NOT BY WORKS OF LAW (Galatians 2:15, 16). Peter not only knew it, says Paul, but believed on Christ in order to be justified. By believing on Christ he repudiated any confidence in the law for justification. His conduct with regard to the Gentiles was thus a blatant nonverbal contradiction of what he both knew and believed.

D. PETER'S CONDUCT AT ANTIOCH IN EATING WITH GENTILE CHRISTIANS WAS INCONSISTENT WITH THE MINISTRY OF CHRIST WHO REMOVED THE LAW AT THE CROSS AND GAVE TO PETER HIS GOSPEL MESSAGE (Galatians 2:17). Peter's nonverbal action, which implied the law was necessary for salvation, also implied that Christ was therefore a minister of sin by removing the law. Paul asks Peter if he is willing to sustain such an indictment against Christ Himself. God forbid! No professing Christian, not even the Judaizers, would make such an indictment. Paul's point in relating this incident about Peter exposes to the Galatians how the legalism of the false teachers contradicts the ministry of Christ and His gospel message of justification by faith.

E. PETER'S CONDUCT WAS INCONSISTENT WITH HIS IM-PLIED INDICTMENT THAT THE GENTILE BRETHREN WERE SINNERS WITHOUT THE LAW (Galatians 2:18). Peter was the sinner at Antioch. He necessarily repudiated the law as essential to salvation when he accepted salvation by faith in Christ. He destroyed whatever confidence he had legalistically in himself to keep the law in order to be saved. But when he separated himself from the Gentiles he reversed his position, he implied the necessity of the law, he implied a repudiation of faith in Christ for salvation, and he built up again what he had earlier destroyed - confidence in himself to keep the law for justification. If he was right in his conduct when he separated from the Gentiles and implied the necessity of the law, then he was wrong when he repudiated the law to become a Christian in the first place. If he was right when he repudiated the law for faith in Christ, then he was wrong when by his conduct he repudiated faith in Christ for the law. Clearly, argues Paul, Peter is the sinner here, not the Gentile brethren.

F. PETER'S SEPARATION FROM THE GENTILES, IMPLYING THE NECESSITY OF THE LAW FOR SALVATION, WAS IN-CONSISTENT WITH THE PURPOSE OF THE LAW (Galatians 2:19). The law was not given for salvation, but to bring men to the realization of their sinfulness, their consequent condemnation, and their human inability to make themselves acceptable to God by keeping the commandments of a law like Moses' law. The law could not offer justification (Galatians 2:16; Acts 13:38, 39), for it is not in the nature of law to justify (Galatians 3:11, 12; Romans 3:19, 20). The purpose of the law was then, and is now, to lead us to Christ (Galatians 3:24) where we can live for God with a clear conscience in spite of our imperfect lives (Hebrews 9:13, 14; 1 Peter 3:21). Men must be educated to the fact that in going to Christ, men die to law as a means of salvation.

G. PETER'S CONDUCT IMPLIED THAT HIS CONFIDENCE WAS IN THE POWER OF HIS OWN FLESH TO MAKE HIMSELF AC-CEPTABLE TO GOD BY LAW KEEPING (Galatians 2:20). This was inconsistent with Christ's vicarious death on our behalf and the gospel of justification by faith in Christ. If men could be saved by keeping the law, Christ would not have had to die.

The law's inability to justify necessitated the death of Christ "for me," that is, on my behalf. From *huper*, *for* means "in behalf of." It is a word of substitution. He "gave Himself *for* our sins" (Galatians 1:4); "Christ died *for* us" (Romans 5:8). He paid the price of our sin, which is death. Isaiah said it clearly:

But He was pierced through for our transgressions, He was crushed for our iniquities; the chastening for our well-being fell upon Him, and by His scourging we are healed. All of us like sheep have gone astray, each of us has turned to his own way; but the LORD has caused the iniquity of us all to fall on Him (Isaiah 53:5, 6).

Mere flesh is impotent to deliver itself from sin's guilt and penalty. But Christ redeemed me by going to the cross. He did for me what I cannot do for myself. He became my sin-offering, my substitutionary sacrifice. By becoming sin on my behalf and dying in my place, He paid the price of my sin. Now God's justice is satisfied. He can justify me, for Christ continues to bear the guilt of my iniquity (Isaiah 53:11; Hebrews 2:17). So Paul says He "delivered Himself up *for* me." That word *for* embraces the incredible love of God and His gift of the atoning sacrifice of Christ on our behalf.

Now the gospel message is that God can justify us on the ground of the cross. That is God's loving response to man. But we are justified by the means of faith, faith that has as its object the person of Christ and His work at the cross. We are to believe on and trust in Christ Jesus. That is man's saving response to God.

When Peter implied that he and the Gentiles were yet answerable to the law, he also implied that the law was the ground of his confidence and that his flesh was the power or means of his justification. This is inconsistent with the gospel. Paul explains that at one time his confidence was also in the law and in his flesh, but that he suffered the loss of all such confidence when he came into the knowledge of the gospel. Now, as a believer in Christ, Paul says he wants only to "be found in him, not having a righteousness of mine own, even that which is of the law, but that which is through faith in Christ, the righteousness which is from God by faith" (Philippians 3:4-9, ASV). The gospel is God's power for the salvation of the believer.

H. FINALLY, PETER'S CONDUCT WAS INCONSISTENT WITH THE UNIVERSAL NEED OF SALVATION BY GRACE AND THE CROSS OF CHRIST (Galatians 2:21). His conduct implied that man could, without help from God, earn his salvation by the power of human flesh through commandment keeping. If Peter's conduct in regard to his Gentile brothers expressed the truth, it would have nullified the need for God's mercy and grace, and the cross of Christ would have been for nought. God forbid!

CONCLUSION: This completes Paul's defense for his divine appointment to the apostleship and for the truth of his gospel. His point in relating Peter's inconsistencies of practice at Antioch was to reflect the inconsistencies of the legalism at Galatia with:

1. trusting in Christ for salvation (Galatians 2:15, 16)
2. the purpose of Christ's ministry (Galatians 2:17)
3. the purpose of the law (Galatians 2:18-19)
4. the power of faith to enable us to live for God (Galatians 2:20)
5. the need for God's grace expressed in the cross (Galatians 2:21)

His logic is incontrovertible. Yet many still pursue the fallacious reasoning of the legalizers. They suppose that to attempt to earn their salvation is somehow praiseworthy and noble, when actually it is vainglorious and impossible. True spiritual character accepts what God offers. One must either receive God's offer of salvation or insult Him.'[2]

Spiritual Probing
Chapter Five

1. Paul's fourth argument for the truth of his gospel was his restatement of his public rebuke of Peter at Syrian Antioch. What was the historical occasion of this rebuke?

2. What did Peter imply regarding the law of Moses when he withdrew from the Gentiles at Antioch? What did he imply regarding those Gentile Christians? What did he imply regarding Christ (Galatians 2:17)? Why was Peter's action hypocritical? To help you answer, look at Galatians 2:15, 16 and ask yourself what it was that Peter knew.

3. Paul tells us that all the Jews at this occasion were carried away with Peter's hypocrisy. Why did Paul single out Peter for the rebuke?

4. Some Bible translations indicate by quotation marks enclosing Galatians 2:14 that Paul's rebuke of Peter begins and ends with verse 14. This means that the rest of Galatians 2:15-21 is spoken directly to the Galatians rather than being Paul's restatement of his rebuke of Peter. What reasoning can you present from that text of the Galatian letter that this entire section (Galatians 2:14-21) is Paul's restatement of his rebuke of Peter?

5. Why did Paul relate his rebuke of Peter to the Galatians?

6. Present the reasoning from Galatians 2:11-14 that Paul is rebuking Peter for gross inconsistency. Can you reason from Galatians 2:3 and 2:14 that Peter's preaching at Jerusalem was inconsistent with his conduct at Antioch? What was Peter compelling the Gentiles to do at Antioch that he did not compel the legalists to do at Jerusalem?

7. What is the force of Paul's argument in Galatians 2:15, 16 as it relates to Peter's inconsistency of belief and conduct?

8. Why did Peter's nonverbal action (not his teaching) reflect upon Christ as a minister of sin (Galatians 2:17)?

9. Who is the real sinner of Galatians 2:18? Why?

10. What did Peter's action imply regarding his own flesh-power and salvation? What did Peter's action deny regarding the death of Christ

in Galatians 2:20? What did Peter's action deny regarding the death of Christ in Galatians 2:21?

11. According to Galatians 2:20, what does legalism imply regarding the power needed to live the Christian life? According to Galatians 2:21, what does legalism deny?

12. According to Galatians 2:20, what is the power to crucify the flesh and to live the victorious Christian life? Harmonize with Galatians 5:25 (Galatians 5:5 and Romans 10:17 can help).

PART TWO:
SCRIPTURAL ARGUMENT
Galatians 3:1-4:31

Chapter Six
Faith, Not Law,
the Means of Our Justification
Galatians 3:1-14

This lesson introduces the second major division of the letter, The Scriptural Division, chapters 3 and 4. Paul dips back into the Hebrew Scriptures no less than nine times to explain to the Galatians that the Old Testament Scriptures themselves teach that we are justified by faith and not by the law of Moses.

The message of this particular lesson (3:1-14) is that we can know we are justified by faith because we have received the gift of the Holy Spirit by faith. Paul takes it for granted that no one can receive the Holy Spirit unless he is already a son of God (4:6). This message is tucked in between two statements of the cross of Christ as the divine ground of our justification (3:1,13). But Paul's emphasis here is that the human means of our justification and reception of the Holy Spirit is faith in Christ, not works of law. He begins by reasoning from several rhetorical questions which he assumes the Galatians will answer on the side of faith and not the law (3:1-5). Next, he reasons from Old Testament Scripture that we are justified by faith, "even as" Abraham was and even as God promised to his seed (3:6-9). Then he reasons from Old Testament Scriptures that we cannot receive the Holy Spirit by works of the law, for even the law itself teaches that no one can be justified by law, but that all men are to be justified by faith (3:10-12). He then concludes that at the cross Christ paid the price of our sin so that we can be justified by faith and as a result receive the indwelling gift of the Holy Spirit (3:13, 14).

The entire section is designed to clarify the fact that only the justified can receive the Spirit, and since the Galatians had already received the Spirit prior to the coming of the Judaizers, the Galatians did not need the law either to be justified or to maintain their justification. The Judaizers' teaching was therefore a basic error inasmuch as it was a rejection of the cross as the foundation of our redemption and faith in Christ as the human response for receiving the Holy Spirit.

I. The Foolishness of Rejecting the Cross For Legalism, 3:1

You foolish Galatians, who has bewitched you, before whose eyes Jesus Christ was publicly portrayed as crucified? (Galatians 3:1).

The sense of the word *foolish*, as a term Paul uses to reflect upon the Galatians' failure in this instance to use their good intellect, is caught in several modern translations. The New English Bible renders it, "You stupid Galatians!" In his new translation, *The Letters And The Revelation*, William Barclay translates, "My Galatian friends, the trouble with you is that you will not use your common sense." Edgar J. Goodspeed's translation is, "You senseless Galatians!" And J.B. Phillips translates, "O you dear idiots of Galatia!" The message comes through that the Galatians were not reasoning sensibly from the implications of the cross of Christ to the means of their justification. As Paul had just pointed out, the reason Christ had to die was because mere human flesh is impotent to atone for sin by any means (2:19-21). Conversely, if we could be justified by mere flesh power through law keeping, then Christ's death was unnecessary. Rather than thinking straight they were seemingly throwing their intellect into neutral as if under a hypnotic trance. If Christ had to die to save us, then the law of Moses, which existed for fifteen hundred years before Christ, simply could not be the means of our salvation.

Barclay's translation in his *Daily Study Bible* for the word *proegraphe* is "placarded": "you before whose very eyes Jesus Christ was placarded upon His Cross?" He says that the Greek word *prographein* was used for putting up a poster, and that it was actually used by a father as a public notice that he would no longer be responsible for his son's debts. Paul reverses the polarity and says that Christ on the cross is like a divine placard notifying the whole world that God our Father has lovingly paid all our debt of sin.

When this good news message is understood, it will be quite clear why Paul said the Galatians were senseless in attempting to pay a debt that they not only could not pay, but that God had already paid the debt for them.

II. Reception of the Holy Spirit Proof of Justification By Faith, 3:2-5

Having indicted the Galatians' acceptance of the law as an unthinkingly foolish contradiction of the message of the cross, Paul now asks four rhetorical questions about their experience with faith and their reception of the Holy Spirit.

This is the only thing I want to find out from you: did you receive the Spirit by the works of the Law, or by hearing with faith? Are you so foolish? Having begun by the Spirit, are you now being perfected by the flesh? Did you suffer so many things in vain - if indeed it was in vain? So then, does he who provides you with the Spirit and works miracles among you, do it by the works of the Law, or by hearing with faith? (Galatians 3:2-5).

The rhetorical nature of the questions clearly assumes that Paul is confident of the Galatians' answers. He is not seeking information by his questions; each question carries its own answer due to their experience with faith.

A. THE ANSWER FROM THEIR CONVERSION EXPERIENCE

"Did you receive the Spirit by the works of the Law, or by hearing with faith?" Paul assumes they would admit they had already received the Spirit when they believed on Christ (3:26, 27; 4:6) prior to the coming of the Judaizers. He also assumes that they know the Holy Spirit is given only to those who are justified (4:6; Acts 2:38; 5:32). If they had received the Spirit, they were therefore justified. What, then, had the Judaizers to offer? The Galatians were already justified. They needed only to see it. So the intent of the question is to lead the Galatians to see that they had already been justified by faith in Christ before the Judaizers arrived in Galatia.

B. THE ANSWER FROM SINFUL FLESH

"Are you so foolish? Having begun by the Spirit, are you now being perfected by the flesh?" Paul contrasts the power of the Spirit with the inability of mere flesh power to complete the Christian's maturing process and finish the journey. The Spirit's power to produce faith in Christ and consequent salvation is the gospel message (Romans 1:16). Earlier in His ministry, Christ promised the apostles a supernatural endowment by the Holy Spirit for special instruction in preaching all things pertaining to the truth of the gospel (John 14:26; 16:13; Acts 1:8). Paul claims that promise was fulfilled when the Holy Spirit provided special revelation to the apostles to "know" the gospel, which to that time was a mystery, hidden by God from before the foundation of the world (1 Corinthians 2:6-12). He goes on to say that the Spirit endowed the apostles to "speak" those "things...not in words taught by human wisdom, but in those taught by the Spirit" (1 Corinthians 2:13). This is condensed in his statement to the Galatians that what he received by revelation he spoke by inspiration (Galatians 1:11, 12). Paul also teaches that we are saved "by the washing of regeneration and renewing by the Holy Spirit" (Titus 3:5). The Spirit's word produces faith, and when faith leads to baptism the Spirit divinely and wonderously generates new life in the believer. Hence, the Galatians began in the Spirit. By apostolic preaching of the gospel the Spirit led them to begin their new life in Christ and renewed them with eternal life.

Paul reasons that since it takes the Spirit's power for sinful men to begin the new life in Christ, does it not also require the same power to complete the journey? Human flesh is at best sinfully imperfect, and under the law that sin would condemn us. If the Spirit had to get us out of sin by the power of the word of the gospel, how foolish is it to think we can stay out of condemnation and grow to Christian maturity by leaving the law of the Spirit of life for a legal system that brings death at the first infraction? The letter kills, but the Spirit gives life.[1]

Paul contrasts faith power with flesh power. We can be saved and matured (perfected) by the Holy Spirit due to what Jesus did for us at the cross. It seems the legalists had no argument with beginning the Christian life by faith. We do not observe these false teachers opposing any effort to bring Gentiles into Christ by gospel preaching and obedience of faith. But not understanding justification by faith, nor the nature of law to condemn us at the next infraction, we observe the Judaizers following behind Paul and attempting to bind the law on newly born Christian Gentiles as essential to perfecting their performance before God (as in Acts 15:1-5). But Paul reminds them that they already have the indwelling Holy Spirit which is received only by sons of God (Galatians 4:6, 7), and are therefore already saved. Consequently they do not need the law to be saved or to complete the journey.

The word *flesh* does not here mean sinful nature, but the power source to complete the Christian life. As Paul explained to the Romans, what the law could not do for us God did through Christ at the cross, "that the requirement of the Law might be fulfilled in us, who do not walk according to the flesh but according to the Spirit" (Romans 8:1-4). In Galatians, to walk by the flesh is to walk by faith in the power of one's own flesh to make oneself acceptable to God. Thus the Judaizer would keep the law in an attempt to establish his own righteousness before God, as in Romans 9:30-10:3. The legalist of today may not bind the law of Moses, but he perverts the works of grace and faith into works of credit and merit and puts faith in his own flesh to perform adequately. As Jesus said, he is trusting in himself that he is righteous (Luke 18:9). To walk by the Spirit is to obey Christ in the confidence that He will do for us what we cannot do for ourselves. To walk by the Spirit is to walk by the Spirit's teaching, which is obedience of faith in Christ (Romans 16:25, 26).

Paul's question, then, was to the point. If it takes Spirit power, gospel power, faith power to begin the Christian life, is it reasonable to think that we can complete the journey by the impotent means of flesh power? If it requires grace by faith to save us, and the Holy Spirit to renew us, can we be brought to Christian maturity by a legal system that would condemn us at the next infraction?

C. THE ANSWER FROM THEIR EXPERIENCE AFTER CONVERSION

"Did you suffer so many things in vain - if indeed it was in vain?" An alternate translation, and perhaps the more accurate rendering is, "Did you **experience** so many things in vain?" Does Paul intend to say that they had suffered for their faith, or is he recalling their experiences of the joy of receiving salvation and the gift of the indwelling Holy Spirit? Such an experience of joy is recalled in Galatians 4:14, 15. The sense in either rendering seems to be that they had not undergone such experiences to no purpose. A moment's reflection would remind the Galatians that their response to the gospel by faith was by no means in vain, for they had received the Holy Spirit who was given only to the justified. Paul assumes they would freely admit this when he earlier asked, "This is the only thing I want to find out from you: did you receive the Spirit by the works of the Law, or by hearing with faith?"

To be consistent we must assume that the Judaizers also would have to admit that the Galatians had received the Holy Spirit. The Judaizers never said that believing Gentiles had not been saved, only that they had to keep the law of Moses and circumcision to maintain their salvation (cf. Acts 15:5). If the Galatians will see the implications of their own answers to Paul's questions, they will have a confirmation of their original faith and a proof of the Judaizers' error.

D. THE ANSWER FROM MIRACLES

"Does He then, who provides you with the Spirit and works miracles among you, do it by the works of the Law, or by hearing with faith?" The Galatians knew that miracles were being performed in their presence. That was a matter of objective observation. The proof of an apostle and the truth of his message were attested by miracles (Mark 16:19, 20; 2 Corinthians 12:12; Hebrews 2:1-4). Earlier, during the Jerusalem conference, Paul and Barnabas had appealed to this same supernaturalism as a divine confirmation of the gospel they preached among the Galatians during their first missionary journey. After returning from their Galatian assignment, they met with the apostles and the church at Jerusalem to defend their gospel against this same legalism. Paul and Barnabas publicly testified that God had confirmed their gospel among the Galatians by "relating what signs and wonders God had done through them among the Gentiles" (Acts 15:12). Paul's statement, then, to the Galatians should be convincing: the miracles that continued among them from the time he first preached the gospel to them once again confirms the truth of his gospel and their own justification prior to the coming of the Judaizers.

The doctrinal inconsistency of the Judaizers is worthy of Paul's indictment of the Galatians' foolishness. Since the Judaizers admit that the Galatians received the Holy Spirit before they came with the law, and since they cannot deny that the confirmation of Paul's gospel by miracles has been in progress at Galatia since before they arrived with the law, then by what reasoning can they conclude that the Galatians would be shut out from salvation without the law (cf. Galatians 4:17), or that Paul's gospel lacked the power to bring men to justification? Paul argues that the gift of the Spirit and the miraculous confirmation of the gospel prior to the coming of the Judaizers precludes the need for the law.

III. We Are Justified By Faith Even As Was Abraham, 3:6-9

Even so Abraham believed God, and it was reckoned to him as righteousness. Therefore, be sure that it is those who are of faith who are sons of Abraham. The Scripture, foreseeing that God would justify the Gentiles by faith, preached the gospel beforehand to Abraham, saying, "All the nations shall be blessed in you." So then those who are of faith are blessed with Abraham, the believer (Galatians 3:6-9).

A. ABRAHAM AN HISTORICAL PRECEDENT, 3:6, 7

Paul appeals to the historical incident of Abraham's justification by faith (Genesis 15:1-6) as a divine precedent: if God can justify one man by faith he can justify all men by faith. On this historical ground we can "know" that we are justified by faith. Paul thus sets it forth that faith is God's abiding principle by which all men have ever been and shall ever be justified. Thus Paul's language, "Even as" Abraham was justified by faith so also are we. The ASV seems to be better since "Even as" separates verses 6-9 from the foregoing, while the NASV, "Even so," makes the content of 6-9 an example of the foregoing. We would punctuate the end of verse 6 with a comma and so make verses 6 and 7 a single sentence, reading, "Even as Abraham believed God and it was reckoned to him as righteousness, therefore be sure that it is those who are of faith who are sons of Abraham."

It should be further observed that since Abraham was justified some five hundred years before the law of Moses was given, that the law of Moses could not be a requirement for justification of Gentiles.

B. GOD'S PROMISE TO JUSTIFY GENTILES BY FAITH, 3:8

Paul tells us that when God promised Abraham that in his seed (offspring) would come the great world-wide blessing (Genesis 12:3), that was God's promise to justify the Gentiles by faith. The "seed" of that promise, says Paul, is Christ (Galatians 3:16), and the "blessing"of that promise is justification by faith (Galatians 3:8). Thus by historical precedent and by divine promise the Scriptures teach that all men for all time will be justified as Abraham was and as God promised, by faith in Christ.

C. PAUL'S CONCLUSION, 3:9

"So then" is Paul's statement of conclusion. If we are "of faith" we will be "blessed" (justified) together with Abraham. The "of faith" stands in contrast to the "of the works of law" in the following verse (3:10) to which the Judaizers subscribed.

IV. Law Not the Ground of Our Justification, 3:10-12

If men are "of faith," that is, if they subscribe to the teaching of justification by faith in Christ, they can be justified. But if they are "of works of law," that is, if they subscribe to the Judaistic teachings of justification by works of law, they cannot be justified. Paul now proceeds in verses 10-12 to explain why this is so.

For as many as are of the works of the Law are under a curse; for it is written, "Cursed is everyone who does not abide by all things written in the book of the law, to perform them." Now that no one is justified by the Law before God is evident; for, "The righteous man shall live by faith." However, the Law is not of faith; on the contrary, "He who practices them shall live by them" (Galatians 3:10-12).

A. THE DOCTRINE OF JUSTIFICATION BY LAW IS CONTRARY TO THE NATURE OF LAW

In this section Paul reasons from the principle to the specific, from the principle that inasmuch as men cannot be justified by law, then specifically they cannot be justified by the law of Moses.

1. **The threefold nature of law**. Paul uses three Old Testament Scriptures to point out the nature of law:

   a. Law requires sinless observance, Galatians 3:12 quoting Leviticus 18:5.

   b. Law condemns the violator, Galatians 3:10 quoting Deuteronomy 27:26.

   c. Law cannot justify the sinner, Galatians 3:11 quoting Habakkuk 2:4.

   The threefold nature of the law of Moses corresponds to the nature of any legal system. Paul applies the principle to the law of Moses. Inasmuch as legal law requires sinless perfection, condemns the violator at the first infraction, and is unable to justify the sinner, therefore the law of Moses cannot be the means of our justification.

   Perhaps the reason for Paul's use of this particular method of reasoning stems from the Galatians' suspicion of his apostolic authority. So he reasons from the principle of the inability of legal law to justify to the inability of the law of Moses to justify. It is apparent he assumes they will understand his method, otherwise such reasoning would be without value. It seems they either knew, or would quickly pick up on the fact, that the nature of legal law renders it unable to justify the sinner. They would be expected, then, to apply this principle to the legal system of Moses' law.

2. **The use and the non use of the definite article**. It will be clear from reading the original that the definite article does not always appear in this section of Galatians before the words "works" and "law." Law without the definite article obviously speaks of the law principle. However, when the definite article precedes the word "law," Paul speaks of a specific law, or

specifically of the law of Moses. The rendering of this section from the original would read more accurately as follows:

For as many as are of works of law are under a curse, for it is written, "Cursed is everyone who does not continue in all things that are written in THE book of THE law to do them." Now that no one is justified by law before God is evident; for, "The righteous man shall live by faith." However, THE law is not of faith.

Paul's method of reasoning here is to appeal to the principle of legal law and then to apply it to the law of Moses by quoting the appropriate Scripture as authority.

B. THE DOCTRINE OF JUSTIFICATION BY LAW IS CONTRARY TO THE PRONOUNCEMENT OF THE LAW

It is important to remember that "those who are of faith are blessed," that is, justified. But "the Law is not of faith," says Paul (Galatians 3:12). Since the law itself says we are justified by faith (Habakkuk 2:4), and inasmuch as the law of Moses is not of faith, we cannot be justified by the law of Moses. The Judaistic doctrine of the necessity of the law for salvation is thus a contradiction of both the nature of the law and the pronouncement of the law itself that it can only condemn sinners.

V. The Cross: The Ground of Our Redemption and of Receiving the Holy Spirit by Faith, 3:13, 14

Christ redeemed us from the curse of the Law, having become a curse for us - for it is written, "Cursed is everyone who hangs on a tree" - in order that in Christ Jesus the blessing of Abraham might come to the Gentiles, so that we would receive the promise of the Spirit through faith (Galatians 3:13, 14).

A. THE PRICE OF REDEMPTION FROM THE LAW'S CURSE

1. **Christ our redeemer**. The word *redeem* comes from the word *agora*, meaning the marketplace where buying and selling transpired. The buying and selling of slaves was a regular feature at the market. The word Paul uses can mean to purchase and so to release a slave from one master to become the property of

another. Involved in the word *redeem* is the idea of cost, a price paid. Paul merges this idea with Christ's cross as the price for our deliverance from Satan's possession that we might become the possession of Christ (cf. Matthew 20:28; Titus 2:14; 1 Corinthians 6:19, 20).

But our deliverance from sin required an unusual price that only Christ was able to pay. The price was a sinless sacrifice to be paid to God for the satisfaction of His justice. Prior to the cross, the devil had the power of death by reason of sin (Hebrews 2:14). "The sting of death is sin, and the power of sin is the law" (1 Corinthians 15:56). But death never got its stinger into Christ, for He remained sinless under the law. Jesus claimed to be stronger than "the strong man," Satan, with the power to bind Satan and to spoil his goods, to carry away his possessions (the souls of men) as booty, as the spoils of war (Matthew 12:29; Luke 11:21, 22). Christ's sinless life under the law showed Him to be stronger than Satan. At the cross Jesus beat the devil out. He bruised the serpent's head (Genesis 3:15), divesting him of his power of death (holding men in separation from God) and bringing deliverance to all the captives who trusted God prior to the cross and since (Hebrews 2:14,15). Hence, "death is swallowed up in victory...thanks be to God, who gives us the victory through our Lord Jesus Christ" (1 Corinthians 15:54, 56). Through faith in Christ, and faithfulness to the death, we also will bruise Satan under our feet shortly (Romans 16:20).

2. **Christ became a curse for us.** To become our Redeemer, Christ had to pay the price of our sin. Sin separates men from God and the law pronounces them worthy of death. But Jesus committed no sin. In what sense, then, could He become a curse? That question is answered in the cross. As Bruce observes, "To be born under law, as he was (4:4), involves no curse, if one keeps the law. And this Christ did....By his lifelong obedience (cf. Romans 5:19) he remained immune from the curse of the law, yet the circumstances of his death brought him unavoidably under the curse. The text which Paul quotes to this

effect had reference originally to the exposure of the corpse of an executed criminal: 'if a man has committed a crime punishable by death, and you hang him on a tree [pole], his body shall not remain all night upon the tree [pole], but you shall bury him the same day, for a hanged man is accursed by God'...(Deuteronomy 21:22f)."[2] Gaebelein also observes that since Jesus "violated the law in one part - through no fault of his own - he became technically guilty of all of it and bore the punishment of God's wrath for every violation of the law by every man...The curse of the law is not a technical, still less an imaginary, thing. The curse is real. Jesus bore this real curse on our behalf.[3] Jesus was literally cursed when He was crucified. Hence His cry from the cross, "My God, my God, why hast thou forsaken me?" God forsook Him that He might not have to forsake us. Praise be to God for His unspeakable gift.

B. THE CURSE TRANSFORMED INTO BLESSING

With the vindication of God's justice and the satisfaction of the law's curse for sin now accomplished at the cross, sinful man can be blessed with justification and receive the gift of the Holy Spirit. Paul explains that this takes place by faith.[4]

CONCLUSION: We are justified today by an obedience of faith even as was Abraham in the long ago. The sole ground of that justification is God's gracious gift of the cross of Christ. Galatians teaches that legalism is a basic error, as it is a rejection of the cross as the only grounds for our redemption and a rejection of faith as the only possible means by which humanity can receive the promised blessing of justification and the gift of the Holy Spirit.

Spiritual Probing
Chapter Six

1. What is the divine ground for our justification? What is the human means of our justification? Can you explain why Paul called the Galatians "foolish" in Galatians 3:1? Do you suppose Christians today might fail to reason from the implications of the cross to their concept and practice of Christianity? Can you illustrate, possibly, from your own experience? Do you suppose some Christians may not know enough about the cross to see its implications upon their lives? Upon legalism?

2. What did Christ accomplish at the cross that makes legalism foolish? Do you suppose Christians can be "bewitched," hoodwinked, mesmerized, by legalism today? Any illustrations? (Keep your answer issue oriented, not person oriented.)

3. Reason from Galatians 3:3 that since it takes Spirit power to start the Christian life (faith in Christ and the regenerating work of the Holy Spirit at baptism, Titus 3:4, 5), it takes the same Spirit power to maintain on-going justification and growth in Christian maturity. Would you say that Spirit power and gospel power are the same? See Romans 1:16, 17.

4. Paul reasons that God's justification of Abraham by faith apart from the law was an historical precedent from which he concludes that all men can be justified by faith apart from law, and that we can "know" it (3:6, 7). By such reasoning we can determine implicit truth even though that truth is not stated explicitly. Jesus elaborated this principle when he said, "You hypocrites! You know how to analyze the appearance of the earth and the sky, but why do you not analyze this present time? And why do you not of your own initiative judge what is right?" (Luke 12:56, 57). He clearly holds humanity responsible to determine certain Christian truths by such reasoning from Scripture facts to conclusions. From what we have studied about the Judaizers' accusations against Paul's authority, why do you suppose Paul used

such reasoning; why did he not rather simply dictate an apostolic doctrine? Can you detect Paul's use of implicit reasoning in other Galatians passages (e.g., 1:11-14; 2:11-18, 21; 3:10-12; 5:2-4)?

5. In Galatians 3:10-12 the threefold nature of law (any legal system) is clearly explained: legal laws (1) require sinless obedience, (2) condemn the violators at the first infraction, and (3) cannot justify the law breakers. Explain how the false doctrine of justification by law is contrary to the threefold nature of law. Explain from the threefold nature of law that the law binders at Galatia understood neither the nature of the law of Moses nor the nature of grace. Do you think Paul's rebuke of such men in 1 Timothy 1:7 applies to those teachers at Galatia? Would they apply to legalists today? How?

6. Do you suppose there are good, conscientious believers in Christ today who do not understand the difference between the law of faith and a law of works? Could these well-meaning brethren, because of that lack of understanding, pervert the new law of the Spirit into a legal system? Do you believe the upshot of such a view could turn faith inward upon oneself to put trust in the wrong person and result in a fall from grace? Can you explain that?

7. Do you think you understand Paul's strategy of reasoning from the principle to the specific? Explain from Galatians 3:10, 11 that Paul is reasoning from the principle that legal law cannot justify to the conclusion that therefore the law of Moses cannot justify. Can you therefore reason that Christianity is not a legal system? What are the wonderful implications of this truth for sinners like us?

8. How could Jesus become a curse for us on the cross when He committed no sin? Paul gave us that answer from Deuteronomy 21:23.

9. Paul says that "Christ redeemed us from the curse of the Law" (Galatians 3:13). The Galatian Gentiles were never under the law of Moses. Before conversion they were pagan idolaters (Galatians 4:8). How, then, could they come under the curse of the law when they were never under the law? Romans 3:19, 20 should give you the answer. Will this help to understand how the law of Moses, though abolished at the cross, yet serves God's wonderful promise to save men by faith in Christ?

10. Paul states in Galatians 3:13, 14 that by faith in Christ we receive (1) the promised blessing of justification and (2) the gift of the Holy Spirit. But on Pentecost Peter taught that we receive remission of sins (the promised blessing) and the gift of the Holy Spirit on the condition of repentance and baptism (Acts 2:38). Can you harmonize Paul's "justification by faith" with Peter's "repent and be baptized for remission of sins"?

The Relation of the Law to the Promise
Galatians 3:15-29

In the preceding lesson, Paul introduced the subject of the Abrahamic promise and proceeded to show that it could not have been fulfilled by the law. He now anticipates the question, What, then, is the purpose of the law? If it cannot bring salvation, why did God give it? Paul answers the question in three parts. He answers first (see I) that God both made and confirmed the promise to Abraham before the law was given, and that neither the fulfillment of the promise nor the condition for its fulfillment could be changed by giving the law later (3:15-18). Next (see II) he explains how the purpose of the law was to prepare humanity to receive the promise (3:19-25). He concludes (see III) that faith, the condition for receiving the promised blessing, expressed in baptism, brings all men to be heirs of the promised blessing (3:26-29).

I. The Giving of the Law Could Not Change God's Confirmed Promise, 3:15-18

Brethren, I speak in terms of human relations: even though it is only a man's covenant, yet when it has been ratified, no one sets it aside or adds conditions to it. Now the promises were spoken to Abraham and to his seed. He does not say, "And to seeds," as referring to many, but rather to one, "And to your seed," that is, Christ. What I am saying is this: the Law, which came four hundred and thirty years later, does not invalidate a covenant previously ratified by God, so as to nullify the promise. For if the inheritance is based on law, it is no longer based on a promise; but God has granted it to Abraham by means of a promise (Galatians 3:15-18).

A. THE FACTS IN THE CASE, 3:15, 16

Note that Paul speaks here of "the promises," plural, that were spoken to Abraham. It is interesting that New Testament writers often refer to the Abrahamic promise as "the promises" (cf. Romans 9:4; 15:8; Galatians 3:21; Hebrews 6:12; 11:13, 17). Since the Abrahamic promise is the mainstream of biblical thought, it has been observed that "the promises" answer to the many Old Testament messianic prophecies that are but different aspects of that single promise made to Abraham. Beecher suggests, "The more adequate idea is not that of many predictions meeting in one fulfillment, but that of one prediction, repeated and unfolded through successive centuries, with many specifications, and in many forms....This is the prevailing note in both Testaments - a multitude of specifications unfolding a single promise."[1]

1. **The promise took the form of a covenant**. About 2000 B.C., God made a promise to Abraham that all families and all nations of earth would be blessed in his seed (Genesis 12:3). Paul quotes this promise twice in Galatians 3:8 and 16, telling us that the seed is Christ (v. 16) and the blessing is justification by faith (v. 8). This promise took the form of a confirmed covenant in Genesis 15:6-18 when the fire of God passed between the sacrificial pieces of the covenant. Later, God confirmed the covenant with an oath, swearing to fulfill it even as He had promised (Genesis 22:16-18; Hebrews 6:13-16).

2. **Paul presents two facts concerning the covenant promise**:

   a. **Fact #1, Confirmed covenants had two characteristics**:

      (1) Confirmed covenants could not be annulled or set aside.

      (2) Confirmed covenants could not have conditions later added as necessary to inherit the estate.

   b. **Fact #2, The promise(s) were made only to Abraham and to Christ his seed.** Paul reasons from the singular number of the word *seed* to clarify that God's promise was not unconditionally inclusive of all of Abraham's physical seed, but rather to Abraham and to Christ alone. His point seems to be aimed at a Judaistic argument that Israelites as the physical offspring of Abraham were ipso facto in line for the promised blessing of justification, and therefore, if Gentiles were to be saved they had to submit to circumcision and the law in order to be eligible for the promise. However, had God indicated a plural number of Abraham's offspring by saying "seeds" rather than "seed," not only would every Jew have been in line for justification by his physical relationship to Abraham, whether he believed in Christ or not, but no Gentile could possibly have been the beneficiary of this particular promise. For, Judaistic argumentation not withstanding, such a promise to "seeds" would have confined the promise to Abraham's physical offspring.

Paul addresses this same topic in Romans. Having detailed the advantages of Israelites to receive God's blessings, among which he mentioned were "the covenants" (seemingly equated with "the promises" of Galatians 3:16), he then clarifies that not all Israelites because they are Abraham's descendants were automatically in line for the promise. He says, "But it is not as though the word of God has failed. For they are not all Israel who are descended from Israel; neither are they all children because they are Abraham's descendants, but: 'Through Isaac your descendants will be named.' That is, it is not the children of the flesh who are children of God, but the children of the promise are regarded as descendants" (Romans 9:6-8). Clearly, then, Jews, simply because they were Jews, were not to be heirs of the promise.

Later Paul will explain that all who are "in Christ" by faith are counted as Abraham's seed and are therefore "heirs according to promise" (Galatians 3:26-29). But for now he wants the Galatians to understand that the Judaizers have not represented the Abrahamic promise correctly.[2]

B. APPLYING THE FACTS, 3:17, 18

Paul's "What I am saying is this" introduces the practical application of the facts regarding the promise.

1. **The law can neither set aside the promise nor be added as a condition to inherit the promise**. The promise preceded the giving of the law by some 500 years. Then, as already noted, God confirmed - ratified - the promise with an oath. Now Paul explains that the law, given some 430 years later, (1) cannot set aside the confirmed promise, (2) nor can the law become a codicil - an added condition - requisite to inherit the promise. That would simply be contrary to God's Word as expressed in the promise and later confirmed in His oath.

2. **The law cannot be the means of receiving the promise**. Again Paul explains: "For if the inheritance is based on law, it is no longer based on a promise; but God has granted it to Abraham by means of a promise." So, God promised to justify us by faith. However, Paul laid it down that, "the Law is not of faith" (3:12). If therefore justification came by the law, as the circumcision party argued, then it would not come by the means of faith as God had promised. This would reflect upon the integrity of God and His immutable Word. Since "it is impossible for God to lie" (Hebrews 6:18), He cannot go back on His promise. So the promised blessing of justification must come by faith and cannot come by law.

It should be a maxim that legalism, ancient and modern, is a misrepresentation of God's promise to save us by faith in Christ as well as a misrepresentation of the nature of law.

II. The Relation of the Law to the Promise, 3:19-25

Why the Law then? It was added because of transgressions, having been ordained through angels by the agency of a mediator, until the seed should come to whom the promise had been made. Now a mediator is not for one party only; whereas God is only one. Is the Law then contrary to the promises of God? May it never be! For if a law had been given which was able to impart life, then righteousness would indeed have been based on law....But before faith came, we were kept in custody under the law, being shut up to the faith which was later to be revealed. Therefore the Law has become our tutor to lead us to Christ, that we may be justified by faith. But now that faith has come, we are no longer under a tutor (Galatians 3:19-21, 23-25).

Paul now anticipates inquiries from the Galatians.

A. WHAT IS THE PURPOSE OF THE LAW? 3:19a

When Paul explains, "It was added because of transgressions," we ourselves may want to ask what that means.

1. **To what was the law added?** Commentators are not agreed whether the law was added to the promise or to something else. It seems from the context that it was added to the promise. Now Paul has already stated that the law could not be added as a condition to receive the promise (3:15). But the same God who gave the promise added the law to serve the promise to its fulfillment, as seen in the following.

2. **The purpose of the law.** Surely Paul intends to convey here the same idea that he so graphically depicted in Romans, that the law's purpose was to thoroughly educate mankind to the exceeding sinfulness of our sin, to our total inability to make atonement for our sins, and therefore to our need for redemption from sin (Romans 3:19, 20; 6:23; 7:13). In this way the law serves the promise. For while the law saves no one, it makes men intensely aware of their inveterate sinfulness and consequent need for justification which comes by faith in Christ. It is not overemphasizing the point to repeat that the same God who gave the promise of justification by faith in Christ also gave the law to serve that promise to its redemptive fulfillment.

B. THE PRIORITY OF THE PROMISE OVER THE LAW, 19b-20

1. **The promise came first.** As already noted, the promise was made and confirmed long before the law was given, and is intended to serve humanity throughout the rest of history. However, the law was only temporary. It was provisional. It would serve only "until the seed should come." While the promise

was given directly to Abraham by God Himself, the law was given by angels through Moses the mediator.

2. **God is one**. The idea of a mediator implies two parties with a third as go-between. This was the case in giving the law, it was "ordained through angels by the agency of a mediator," that is, Moses. But in the case of the promise to Abraham it came directly from God. Now God is but one party, and there was no third party as mediator between God and Abraham when God made the promise to him.

The priority of the promise over the law is unquestionable. The promise came first, is permanent, and was delivered by God Himself. But the law came much later, is servant to the promise, was temporary, was merely provisional, and was given by angels through Moses, a human mediator.

C. WAS THE LAW CONTRARY TO THE PROMISES? 3:21-25

"Is the Law then contrary to the promises of God? May it never be!" Paul is indignant. He knows that the same God who gave the promise gave the law to serve the promise to its fulfillment. The law served the promise in the following ways:

1. **The law makes men understand that salvation comes only by the means promised, by faith** (Galatians 3:21b-23). As already noted, the purpose of the law was to educate men to the fact that they are condemned sinners and that no one can be justified by a legal system. This leads naturally to justification by faith: "But the Scripture has shut up all men under sin, that the promise by faith in Jesus Christ might be given to those who believe."

2. **The law served as a *paidagogos*** (Galatians 3:24, 25). The word *tutor* falls quite short of the original meaning, as does *schoolmaster* and *custodian*. There is simply no English equivalent.

The *paidagogos*, literally a boy-leader, was usually a man.[3] "Paidagogos, a guide, or guardian of boys, lit., a child-leader...In this and allied words the idea is that of training, discipline, not of impartation of knowledge. The paidagogos was not the instructor of the child; he...was responsible for his moral and physical well-being. Thus understood, paidagogos is appropriately used with 'kept in ward' and 'shut up' whereas to understand it as equivalent to 'teacher' introduces an idea entirely foreign to the passage."[4]

"In the Graeco-Roman world, the child-custodian (pedagogue), or attendant, fulfilled certain clearly defined functions. He was often a slave appointed by the parent to conduct the child to school and to have general charge of him until he came of age, even to imparting ethical instruction to him. If the child must travel abroad for his education, it was the attendant's responsibility to put him under a suitable teacher. Competent attendants were highly esteemed by parents, and children were required to respect them."[5]

The point Paul is making is that the law can never bring men to spiritual maturity to receive the promised blessing of justification. Only faith can do that. So Paul concludes, "But now that faith has come, we are no longer under a [paidagogos]."

3. **The law led us to the faith** (Galatians 3:23-25). Understanding these three sentences lies in Paul's use of the definite article before the word *faith*, as in the following:

But before faith came, we were kept in custody under the law, being shut up to THE faith which was later to be revealed. Therefore the Law has become our tutor to lead us to Christ, that we may be justified by faith. But now that faith has come, we are no longer under a tutor.

Paul's generic use of the word "faith" without the definite article refers to the human means of access to God, as in verse 24, "that we may be justified by faith." This use of *faith* refers to the act of believing. But this is not the meaning of "the faith." By "the faith" Paul means the thing believed, the Christian faith, the authoritative teaching of the apostles of justification by faith in Christ. This is in contrast to "the law." This is the "one faith" by the knowledge of which, Paul says, we all attain to Christian unity (Ephesians 4:4, 13). The singularity of "the faith" distinguishes it from any other belief system. Here

Paul particularizes the law system of Moses. The Christian faith is distinctive, identifiable. It can be preached, believed, obeyed - we can strive for it and contend for it (cf. Acts 6:7; 13:8; 14:22; Galatians 1:23; Philippians 1:27; 1 Timothy 4:1; Jude 3). This is "the faith" that after the law had served its purpose, was "later to be revealed." And after Christ abolished the law at the cross "the faith" was later revealed at Pentecost.

Paul's point is that the law of Moses was provisional and temporary; it served the promise to its fulfillment in Christ, and was then removed (Galatians 3:25). Now we are under the "law of faith" (Romans 3:27), "under the law of Christ" (1 Corinthians 9:21) that teaches we are justified by faith in Christ.

III. Faith the Means of Sonship and Inheritance, 3:26-29

For you are all sons of God through faith in Christ Jesus. For all of you who were baptized into Christ have clothed yourselves with Christ. There is neither Jew nor Greek, there is neither slave nor free man, there is neither male nor female; for you are all one in Christ Jesus. And if you belong to Christ, then you are Abraham's offspring, heirs according to promise (Galatians 3:26-29).

A. IDENTIFYING THE TRUE FAMILY OF GOD, 3:26, 27

About 2000 B.C. God made the promise to Abraham that through his seed would come the special blessing of salvation to all nations (Genesis 12:3; 22:18; Galatians 3:8, 16). God then made a special covenant with Abraham's seed to be their God. As a consequence, at birth the Hebrew became a covenant-related child of God (Genesis 17:1-14). About 1500 B.C. God made a covenant with Israel as a nation to become His own special people (Exodus 19:1-24:9; 34:27, 28). Indeed Israel was distinctive. Her religio-legal economy was unique in the earth. She was set apart from the rest of the nations as a special people chosen of God, with circumcision as the divine token of that relationship. This special relationship was for a special purpose - the bringing of the Messiah, Abraham's seed, into the world. Before Israel was a nation, indeed before time began, God intended to expand His family through the Messiah to include all nations. He would accomplish this through Christ and the cross and the gospel of justification by faith.

With the coming of the Messiah, Israel and the law had served the promise to its fulfillment. Though the principles of righteousness and morality enunciated in the law remain - even as they existed prior to giving the law - the law as a legal system of national governance was abolished at the cross (Ephesians 2:15). Since the cross, Israel, having served her Messianic purpose, is no longer specially related to God as the theocratic nation either by national covenant, by Abrahamic lineage, or by divine promise. God's new family, the church, according to the Abrahamic promise, includes people of all nations, and became the new theocratic nation (1 Peter 2:9), His special family by faith in Christ. In Galatians 3:26-29 Paul redefines the identity of God's new family.

1. **Sons of God by faith in Christ**. In the Greek New Testament the words for *sons* and *children* are different words conveying a different status for each. Children are under guardianship; they are not of an age to inherit the father's estate (Galatians 4:1-3). They have neither the legal status nor the privilege of full-grown sons (Galatians 3:26; 4:5, 6). The teaching of Galatians 3:26-29, that we become sons of God and heirs of the promise by faith in Christ at baptism, grows out of this figure of a child coming of age and receiving the inheritance.

2. **Sons of God by faith at baptism**. At baptism, Paul says, our faith makes us full-grown sons, heirs of the blessing of justification.

    a. **The Greek word for baptism is *baptizo***. As used in both New Testament and non-Christian literature the word means to dip, immerse, plunge, sink. We should think of this baptism in water as a command to be obeyed to become a son of God. This is distinct from the baptism of the Holy Spirit which was a promise of empowerment for a select few in the first century. We don't obey promises, we obey commands. The word *baptism* is clearly not a translation corresponding to this definition. *Baptism*, from *baptizo*, is more like a transliteration in which the sound is transposed into the vernacular. In point of fact the word *baptism* has no distinctive meaning outside of a theological or church context. *Baptism* today is thought of in terms of sprinkling, or pouring water on one's head, and sometimes immersion. It should have been translated in our modern Bibles to correspond with the first century vernacular meaning as defined in the lexicons. When Christ and the apostles commanded "baptism," they actually commanded immersion in water. This is not a matter of interpretation, but of lexical definition. Thus Paul reminded the Ephesians how they were "cleansed...by the washing [a bath] of water with the word" (Ephesians 5:25, 26), and how Paul himself was commanded to "Arise and be [immersed], and wash away thy sins" (Acts 22:16, ASV).

b. **The purpose of Christian baptism**. According to the New Testament writers' own statements of its purpose, baptism, preceded by repentance, is an expression of faith in Christ to receive the forgiveness of sins (Acts 2:38; 1 Peter 3:21) and to bring us into union with Christ (Romans 6:1-7). It has already been mentioned that the Lord's command to be baptized "in the name of the Father and the Son and the Holy Spirit" (Matthew 28:19), or, which is the same, "in the name of the Lord Jesus" (Acts 8:16; 19:5; 1 Corinthians 1:13), means "into the possession" of Christ. It is, then, at baptism that the lost sinner is united with Christ as His own possession.

Paul reminds the Romans of their baptism "into Christ," "into His death," in order to be raised from the dead in sin and walk in newness of the Christian life. In baptism, says Paul, "we have become united with Him in the likeness of His death" so that "we shall be also in the likeness of His resurrection" (Romans 6:1-7).

Paul did not have to educate the Galatians to the doctrine of baptism, nor did he have to elaborate its purpose inasmuch as it was not an issue with the Galatians. He but recalled what he had earlier taught them and how all of them were by faith "baptized into Christ." Paul's point is that since the Galatians became sons of God, clothing themselves with Christ's righteousness as a garment, they should know that neither law nor circumcision was needed to maintain their family membership with God.

c. **Baptism is an act of the alien sinner's faith in Christ to forgive him**. "For you are all sons of God through faith in Christ Jesus. For all of you who were baptized into Christ have clothed yourselves with Christ." Baptism is an act of faith in Christ to be forgiven and become one with Him. It is Christ who has commanded baptism into His possession (Matthew 28:19). It is Christ who said that he that believes the gospel and is baptized shall be saved (Mark 16:15, 16). Baptism is not legalism; it earns us nothing. It is a condition of faith's trust in Christ to forgive us at the point of baptism as He said He would. The apostles conveyed that message when they preached the gospel (Acts 2:38; 8:12, 16; 10:48; 16:14, 15, 30-34; 19:1-5; 22:12-16).

Paul teaches that baptism is the expression of the sinner's faith in Christ to cut away his sins (Colossians 2:11, 12). Baptism is not spiritual circumcision, but the moment in time when God cuts away our sins. Paul, using the analogy of circumcision, clearly defines the "circumcision made without hands" as "the putting off of the body of the sins of the flesh." He then explains that in baptism God spiritually circumcises the sinner of his sins: "having been buried with Him in baptism, in which you were also raised up with Him through faith in the working of God." What is baptism? It is faith in God Who works at cutting away sin as He said He would when we are baptized.

Luke relates for us the very informative and important account of certain "disciples" of John's baptism that were at Ephesus, who had not been baptized into the name of the Lord Jesus (Acts 18:24-19:5). Consequently they were neither the possession of the Lord nor were they in possession of the indwelling Holy Spirit. This indwelling of the Holy Spirit is highly significant to our salvation, inasmuch as it is also true that "if any one does not have the Spirit of Christ, he does not belong to Him" (Romans 8:9). And it is also true that only those whose sins have been forgiven and who are thus sons of God can receive the Holy Spirit (Acts 2:38; Galatians 3:26, 27; 4:5). Thus, in conversation with these disciples Paul was stimulated to ask, "Did you receive the Holy Spirit when you believed?" They answered that they had not so much as heard if there was a Holy Spirit. Immediately Paul responded: "Into what then were you baptized?" He didn't ask if they had been baptized. That was assumed. His question was, "Into what then were you baptized?" Paul asked the question because he could not separate baptism into the name of the Lord (into the possession of the Lord) from belief in Christ and the reception of the Holy Spirit, which is essential to belong to Christ and to be saved. When Paul explained that John's baptism was unto repentance rather than by faith in Christ, "they were baptized in the name of the Lord Jesus." Into what were they baptized? Into the possession of the Lord. At that point in time they became the possession of Christ and received the indwelling Holy Spirit (Acts 19:1-5).[6] The supernatural empowering of these new Christians by the laying on of Paul's apostolic hands was manifested in their speaking in tongues and prophesying (Acts 19:6-7). Thus we observe the difference between receiving the indwelling Holy Spirit at baptism, which obtains today, and the empowering by the Holy Spirit of first century Christians by the imposition of apostolic hands.

d. **Baptism is to "put on Christ".** As the Roman youth put on his toga, the sinner in baptism puts on Christ. "This is a favorite metaphor of Paul's (cf. Romans 13:12; Ephesians 4:24; Colossians 3:12)...But here (and in Romans 13:14) is his most daring use of it, in which he likens Christ himself to a garment. The expression conveys a striking suggestion of the closeness which exists between Christ and the believer. Those who put on Christ can do no other than act in accordance with the spirit of Christ...the metaphor conveys an essentially new kind of life."[7] Baptism, then, is the place where the old man of sin discards the clothing of his former sinful life, and wherein he is clothed with Christ for the new life.

"This close relationship which baptism establishes between Christ and the believers is also designated by the expression: baptized into Christ...The baptized person is added to Christ as His own, is reckoned to His account, shares in His benefits. And the closeness of the relationship is confirmed by the exegetical expression: to put on Christ. Just as a garment which one puts on...quite envelops the person wearing it, and identifies his appearance and his life, so the person baptized into Christ is quite entirely taken up in Christ and in the salvation brought by Him."[8] Ridderbos footnotes the comment that "to put on Christ" becomes the equivalent of..."putting on the new man" (Colossians 3:10; Ephesians 4:24).

We should not speak of "Paul's interpretation of baptism," as if there is a different interpretation that holds equal authority with his. Baptism into Christ to put on Christ is not Paul's interpretation. It is the very word of God which Paul received by special revelation (1 Corinthians 2:12, 13; 11:23a). The baptism of which Paul speaks is the baptism Christ commanded men to administer to non-covenant related men who are ready to become Christ's covenant possession (Matthew 28:19). There is only "one baptism" (Ephesians 4:4, 5). It is the baptism that Christ and the apostles commanded men to administer to other men when faith is ready to obey the Lord by immersion in water to become sons of God. We are all baptized by one

Spirit into one body when faith in Christ obeys the Spirit's word to be baptized to become sons of God (1 Corinthians 12:13). This baptism is not an unseen action of the Spirit, as if it were spiritualized into invisibility to mean something other than what Paul and the other inspired men of the New Testament teach that it means - immersion in water "in the name of Jesus Christ for the forgiveness of your sins" (Acts 2:38). New Testament baptism must not be spiritualized away to mean something other than immersion in water to become saved sons of God. Baptism as an expression of faith in Christ to save renders that faith perfected, and that faith, says James, is reckoned for righteousness (James 2:20-23).

"The 'baptism into Christ' refers back to 'faith in Christ' in verse 26. In both, there is a conscious act, for the Greek verb about their baptism is in the middle voice, so as to express the fact that they had themselves baptized, as they themselves had believed."[9]

Any theology of baptism that attempts to place the alien sinner in Christ and therefore saved prior to baptism does not represent God's revelation of the subject as Paul "delivered" it. He says that we clothe ourselves with Christ when faith leads us to obey Him by being baptized into Christ. Nowhere does the New Testament say that baptism is an outward picture that the Holy Spirit has already baptized us into Christ. Scripture is not correctly represented when it is taught that baptism is an outward expression of an inward grace that God has already saved us by faith alone.

B. FAITH DOES NOT DISCRIMINATE, 3:28

There is neither racial (Jew or Gentile), social (slave or free), or sexual (male or female) discrimination against any person exercising his or her faith to be justified. In the Roman world of Paul's day, the Greeks divided all men into two classes, Greeks and barbarians. The Jews considered themselves the elite and called all others goyim, the hordes of heathen nations (Gentiles) in contrast to Israel. A Jew's prayer would sometimes include his gratitude that God had not made him a Gentile, a slave, or a woman. A woman was considered the property of her husband, and her status ranked with slaves and children. "In every respect woman is inferior to man," said Josephus (Against Apion, II. 24). Aristotle defined a slave as "an animated implement."[10]

But faith at baptism identified a Gentile slave girl as Christ's, as a seed of Abraham, and therefore as surely and quickly saved as a free Jewish male. By faith in Christ at baptism, the commonality of Christianity becomes a reality with God and with all who understand that every individual stands before God justified by grace. There is no place in Christ for racial, social, or gender elitism, or for haughty intellectual exclusivism. For in Christ we are all one man.

Unfortunately this statement has been misused by accomodating the language of the text to a theology of the role of women in leadership and in the assembly that is in opposition to very clear apostolic teaching. It is claimed that Galatians 3:28 authorizes Christian women to participate in the leadership roles of the church and in the assembly that have been "traditionally" confined to men, and therefore they can teach, preach, and lead in public prayer in the worship assembly. However, there is nothing about leadership that is inherent in Paul's statement, or the role of men or women in worship. Paul is very plainly saying that women have equal access to justification by faith in Christ as males do, and that therefore Christian men and women "are one man in Christ," that is, one body of redeemed humanity. This statement of God's acceptance of women, elevating them to the highest possible level of human attainment - the status of children of God with all rights and privileges to that relationship - manifests their equality before God in relation to their humanity. This statement, among others (e.g. Ephesians 5:25-30), lifted women from their second class citizenship (to which they were assigned in the second century) to a human status equal with men in the sight of God and His church.

However, Paul's "one man in Christ" does not cancel out his apostolic instruction that the wife is to submit to her husband, or that the husband is the head of the wife (Ephesians 5:22-32). While the husband has no authority to subjugate his wife, she is instructed to place herself willingly in submission to him. This is not the husband's right, but her assignment because of her relationship to Christ as Lord. But in this relationship they are still "one man in Christ," having equal access to God's justification by faith.

Paul's reasons and instruction regarding the silence of women in the Christian assembly are explicit:

Let the women keep silent in the churches; for they are not permitted to speak, but let them subject themselves, just as the Law also says. And if they desire to learn anything, let them ask their own husbands at home; for it is improper for a woman to speak in church (1 Corinthians 14:34, 35).

The suggestion that this instruction is required of Christian women in a particular culture that is not applicable to us does not seem to respect the universality of the language of the text. Paul says this instruction is in agreement with what is to be practiced in "all the churches of the saints" (1 Corinthians 14:33). This lifts the teaching out of a mere cultural requirement at Corinth to an obligation among all churches of Christ world-wide. Further, Paul lends Old Testament authority to his instruction by stating that such silence in the assemblies was practiced under the law.

Paul gave the same basic instruction to Timothy to be preached in the church at Ephesus (1 Timothy 2:8-12) and explained that this doctrine was inherent in God's order of creation - man first, then woman - and due to the woman's behavior when beguiled by the serpent.

For Adam was first formed, then Eve; and Adam was not beguiled, but the woman being beguiled hath fallen into transgression (1 Timothy 2:13, 14, ASV).

The word *for*, expressing cause, conveys the reason or the proof that the foregoing statement is true. Why did Paul teach that men (*andras* from *aner*, distinguishing men from women) and not women were to pray in mixed gender meetings of the church, and why did Paul not permit the women to teach or have dominion over men? Paul's reasons had nothing to do with cultural requirements, but were inherent in the actions of God and Adam and Eve from the beginning of creation.

C. BELIEVERS IN CHRIST BECOME HEIRS OF THE PROMISE, 3:29

"And if you belong to Christ, then you are Abraham's offspring, heirs according to promise." There is a spiritual fact that God accepts, but that escapes reason's ability to explain - that Christians are somehow the true seed of Abraham because they are Christ's. This is no easier to explain than how it is that God accepts Christ's suffering as payment for our sin-debt. Why? By what logic can we explain that a sinner's faith in Christ makes him or her the seed of Abraham? But explain it or not, it is a glorious fact of revelation. Thank God for His unspeakable gift.

CONCLUSION: The same God that gave the promise gave the law. His great purpose for the law was to serve the promise to its fulfillment for our sakes. The law accomplished this by enlightening men to the fact that we are all inveterate sinners and that we are totally incapable of making ourselves right with God apart from the cross of Christ. In this way we see the law was not contrary to the promise, but as a servant it led men to realize their need for Christ.

Those who would trust Christ and put Him on in baptism become sons of God and receive the indwelling gift of the Holy Spirit. These experience the triumph of freedom from sin and the condemnation of law.

Spiritual Probing
Chapter Seven

1. Paul speaks of God's great promise of justification by faith as a confirmed covenant. Then he explains that confirmed covenants had two characteristics (apparently well known to the Graeco-Roman world): (1) they could not be set aside, (2) nor could they later have other conditions added as necessary for inheritance. How did Paul expect these characteristics to be applied to the law and to the promise? You can get started with Galatians 3:17, 18.

2. God made a promise to justify us by faith (Genesis 12:3; Galatians 3:8). Do you suppose God would promise to justify men by one means and then justify them by a different means? What does Galatians 3:22 say about this? But the law-binders at Galatia were teaching that men were justified by law (Galatians 5:4). Were they not teaching contrary to the promise? Inasmuch as Paul says that "the Law is not of faith" (Galatians 3:12), what does that necessarily imply regarding the Judaizers' knowledge of the law of Moses? First Timothy 1:7 is a very appropriate comment on the law-binders at Galatia and on legalism today.

3. As a follow-up to the above question, consider that Paul, speaking of the principle of legal law (not speaking directly of the law of Moses), said we are not justified by law (Galatians 2:16), nor are we under law (Romans 6:14). Yet in 1 Corinthians 9:21 he said, "we not being without the law of God but under the law of Christ." Harmonize these important statements by explaining (1) the difference between a legal law (like Moses' law) and the law of faith, and (2) the kind of law Christians are under.

4. But if law cannot be the means of our justification (Galatians 3:11), then what was God's purpose for giving the law of Moses? See Galatians 3:19a, 22. Can you explain how the law serves the promise to its fulfillment? Does the law of Moses still serve the promise? If so, how? If not, why? Romans 3:31 might help.

5. What is the real meaning of Paul's analogy that the law is like a tutor? Does that word *tutor* really express the first-century meaning of the Greek word *paidagogos*? What is the meaning of the word *paidagogos*, and in what way does Paul relate it to the law's purpose to lead men to Christ?

6. Paul uses a word for sons that is distinct from the word for children. Each word conveys a different status in relation to the family in the Graeco-Roman world. Explain the status of sons in contrast to the status of children. Then explain how Paul intended this analogy to be applied to the law and to the promise of justification in Galatians 3:26, 27 and 4:1-3.

7. Paul says in Galatians 3:28 there is no male and female in Christ. Is this speaking of women's role in the church, or of justification by faith? Is he saying that Gentile slave girls can be justified as surely as Jewish free-men, or is he speaking of women's rights to lead prayer in the public assembly? If the latter is true, would this not contradict Paul's statements in 1 Corinthians 14:33-37 and 1 Timothy 2:8-14?

8. What is the definition of the Greek word *baptizo* that is translated baptize? If the Bible teaches that at baptism we are saved (Mark 16:16; 1 Peter 3:21), transferred into the possession of Christ (Matthew 28:19), forgiven (Acts 2:38), brought into union with Christ (Romans 6:3-5), made to be sons of God and heirs of the promise (Galatians 3:26, 27), can an alien sinner be saved without baptism? If so, would that not be tantamount to saying that God promised to save us one way, but will save us another way? Would that reflect on the reliability of God's Word? How?

9. We are saved by faith, but we are saved at the point of baptism. Explain the relationship of baptism to justification by faith. Galatians 3:26, 27; Acts 19:1-5; Colossians 2:11, 12 will help.

Legal Law Makes Slaves of Sons
Galatians 4:1-11

The word *heirs* is the connecting link between the close of Galatians three and the beginning of chapter four. Paul picks up from his concluding statement that, "if you belong to Christ, then you are Abraham's descendants, heirs according to promise," and transitions into an explanation that Christ's birth under the law was for the purpose of redeeming Israel from the law's enslavement to sin (4:1-5). He further explains that if these Galatian Gentile Christians, who were freed from their former bondage to sin under idolatry, placed themselves under the law they would commit spiritual suicide. For the law would condemn them at their next infraction as surely as it did the Jews. They would return to bondage to sin inasmuch as the law could not free them from sin anymore than it could free Israel (4:6-11). Paul makes it clear, that whether Jews or Gentiles, the law cannot produce heirs to the Abrahamic promise; it can only produce slaves to sin.

I. Israel in Bondage Under the Law, 4:1-3

Now I say, as long as the heir is a child, he does not differ at all from a slave although he is owner of everything, but he is under guardians and managers until the date set by the father. So also we, while we were children, were held in bondage under the elemental things of the world (Galatians 4:1-3).

A. PAUL'S ANALOGY, 4:1, 2

Paul appeals to the well-known practice of a minor son who, though "he is owner of everything" from infancy, has no authority or control over his estate until he reaches the age set by his father. During the interim, as a minor, he is actually like a slave over whom others have authority and control.

B. THE ANALOGY APPLIED TO JEWS UNDER THE LAW FOR THE GALATIANS' SAKE, 4:3

Paul's point is that since the Jews were in bondage under the law the Galatians in like manner would be in bondage under the law.

1. **"We," that is, Jews**. The "we" cannot properly embrace Christian Gentiles in their former life. The plural pronouns "we," "you," and "our" distinguish between "we" Jews, who under the law were children but whom Christ made sons, and "you" Galatian Christians who "are sons" (as previously stated in Galatians 3:26). And now because "we" Jews and "you" Gentiles are sons, God sent forth the Spirit of His Son into "our" hearts.

2. **Defining "bondage."** To what were the Jews in bondage while under the law?

   a. **Mere enslavement to Jewish ritual**? Advocates of the Calvinistic theology of the impossibility of apostasy speak here of keeping the law as if it were drudgery. Since they cannot believe the justified can lose their salvation, they must view the adoption of law keeping as in some sense pejorative, though not spritually fatal. But David praised the law, saying, "O how I love thy law! It is my meditation all the day," and, "thy law is my delight" (Psalm 119:97, 77). Did David delight in drudgery? Were the Israelites worn down by sabbath keeping, which was imposed for the benefit of men that they not be overworked? Were keeping the commandments and the ordinances of Moses' law and the civil and ceremonial ordinances drudgery? Not to those whose hearts were attuned to God. There was nothing wrong with the law itself. It was "perfect" (Psalm 19:7). The law's ritual was not a curse, but a blessing. However, it exposed mankind's utterly sinful nature, pronounced him a bond-slave to sin, and revealed his inability to save himself by such a legal system. It was when men perverted the nature of the law into legalism, as these false teachers had done, and attempted to be justified by law keeping that it became an unbearable "yoke" (Acts 15:10).

b. **Bondage under the law**. Paul is very explicit that those who appeal to the works of the law as a means of justification are "cursed" by the law. This is due to the fact that none are righteous of ourselves, we all have sinned, and even Christians who "walk in the Light" ever so sincerely are not without sin (Psalm 143:2; Romans 3:23; 1 John 1:7-8). And it is further a fact, explains Paul, that the law cannot free us from the guilt and penalty of our sin. Instead it holds us guilty with every infraction. That is the nature of a legal system. Paul strains in Galatians to make that clear, and that therefore Christ came to redeem us from the curse of the law (3:13). At the moment men are cursed under the law for their sin they are "held in bondage" by the law to the guilt and penalty of their sin (4:3).

But the question rises: What is that "bondage," that enslavement? Is it merely bondage to the drudgery of observing the ritual of the law? Or is it bondage to sin and death, separation from God even for Christians for whose sin- guilt the law of Moses cannot set us free (cf. Galatians 3:22)? Paul's point in Galatians 3:10-13 is that the law can justify no one in his bondage to sin; it can only pronounce the curse of death upon all who violate it, and it is this curse of the law from which Christ went to the cross to deliver us. He did not die merely to deliver us from the drudgery of law keeping. He died to deliver us, alien sinners and Christians, from the bondage of sin and death.

In the context of Galatians 4:3 the "bondage" to which the Jews were held is the bondage to sin and death from which the "elemental things" of the law can set no one free. The works of the law of Moses, which Paul styles "the elemental things of the world," that is, the law's ritual, cannot free either the alien sinner or the Christian from the guilt and enslavement of his sin. The works of the law were not given to atone for sin. Sin produces bondage and the "elemental things" of the law are exposed as "weak and worthless," totally unable to free the alien sinner or the Christian from the guilt and penalty of his sin (4:9). Paul teaches that to accept the law is to accept a system that can no more free men from their bondage to sin than it could mature Jews out of their spiritual childhood and transform them into the full age of "sons" to inherit the promise of justification. To appeal to the law for salvation, and thus in principle to any legal system, is but to place oneself in bondage to the guilt and penalty of his sin from which the weak and worthless rituals of that system can free no one.

c. **The terms "slavery" and "freedom" are used antithetically** (Galatians 2:4; 5:1). Paul's "slavery " is slavery to the law of Moses that by its nature cannot free the violator from the guilt and penalty of his sin. In principle this slavery is to any religious system of law that by its nature cannot free the alien sinner or the Christian from sin guiltiness. When the law of liberty is viewed as a legal system, and when its works of grace and faith are legalistically perverted into works of credit and merit, the Christian will naturally turn his trust inward upon himself, and place himself under a yoke of bondage that cannot free him from the guilt of his next sin.

Paul's "freedom" is freedom from the guilt and penalty of sin. The Galatians were freed from their bondage to sin when by faith they were baptized into Christ. These Gentiles were never under the law of Moses to have been liberated from it. Their former bondage was to sin under idolatry. When they believed the gospel they were liberated from the curse of sin that the law pronounced upon all sinners (cf. Galatians 3:13; Romans 3:19; 1 Timothy 1:8-11). Paul's point to the Galatians is that if the Jews were in bondage to sin under the law, these Galatian Christians would likewise be in bondage to sin under the law. When Paul writes, "how is it that you turn back again to the weak and worthless elemental things, to which you desire to be enslaved all over again," he does not say these Gentile Christians had turned back to the law. They were never under the law to turn back to it. But if they placed themselves under the law, as false teachers were encouraging them to do, they would return to condemnation by the law at their next infraction. The law, implies Paul, has no more power to liberate men from sin and death than does pagan idolatry.

3. **"The weak and worthless elemental things of the world**." This is also translated "worldly rudiments" or "worldly principles." The Greek word *stoicheia* meant the elementary rudiments of any branch of learning. The word means things arranged in a row or side by side as the letters of the alphabet, the ABCs. Bruce observes, and it seems correct, that "since the letters of the alphabet were regarded as the 'elements' of which words and sentences are built up, stoicheia comes to be used of the 'elements' which make up the material world (cf. 2 Peter 3:10, 12). This would be the natural sense of the rudiments of the world unless the context dictated otherwise...but in the immediate context existence under the rudiments of the world is equated with existence under law (Galatians 4:4f.). He speaks of the time during which the people of God lived 'under law' as the time they spent in the infant class learning their ABCs - which for them amounted to 'the rudimentary notions of the world.'[1]

These "worldly rudiments" are defined in verses 9 and 10 as the "weak and worthless elemental things" of the law of Moses, such as ritual observance of "days and months and seasons and years." *Worldly* is used to mean "of this material world" - not evil things, but mere things of the world, like sabbath and circumcision and animal sacrifice. These cannot take away sin. Nor can any such worldly rudiments that men have invented to themselves, says Paul. They are of "no value" (Colossians 2:20-23). To engage in such ritual for salvation is "vain" (Galatians 4:11). Such ritual, whether of the law of Moses or the "precepts and doctrines of men" are too weak before God to take away sin and are thus "worthless" before God to save sinners. Obviously these can no more take away sin than could the pagan ritual of their former idolatry. Consequently if the Galatians accepted the law as an essential access unto God then they, too, would come under the law's curse and return to the bondage of sin and death to which they were held captive under pagan idolatry. Thus Paul states, "But now that you have come to know God, or rather to be known by God, how is it that you turn back again to the weak and worthless elemental things [of Jewish ritual] to which you desire to be enslaved all over again?" (4:9). Paul does not say these Galatian Christians were returning to the law. They were never under the law to return to it. But by accepting the law they would return to a ritual that was as weak and worthless as the ritual of their former pagan idolatry that could no more free them from sin than could the law of Moses free the Jews. In effect, if they accepted the law, they would return to the bondage of their sins from which the ritual of the law could not set them free.

II. God Makes Us Sons and Heirs, 4:4-7

But when the fullness of the time came, God sent forth His Son, born of a woman, born under the Law, that He might redeem those who were under the Law, that we might receive the adoption as sons. Because you are sons, God has sent forth the Spirit of His Son into our hearts, crying, "Abba! Father!" Therefore you are no longer a slave, but a son; and if a son, then an heir through God (Galatians 4:4-7).

It must be remembered that salvation is of God. Man in his perversion often throws the human and the divine parts out of proportion to the disparagement of the divine and the exaltation of the human. But Paul artfully shows that the beginning and the end of our redemption is a thing of God. He tells us who came, Christ Jesus; when He came, in the fullness of the time; how He came, born of a woman, born under the law; and why He came, to redeem us from slavery to sin and to adopt us as sons into His own divine family. It is God who makes us His sons. It is God who sends us His Spirit. We are therefore heirs, says Paul, "through *God.*"

A. THE FULLNESS OF THE TIME

This expression, "But when the fullness of the time came," is in line with the analogy Paul used in Galatians 4:1-3 of the date set by the father for his son to inherit the estate. And even as fathers set the date for that inheritance years ahead of time, so in His eternal purpose, before time began, God set the time for the coming of His Son to redeem men from sin. When Christ appeared on the historical scene, it was the fullness of the time. Donald Guthrie's observation is to the point:

"What caused Paul to use this expression here? The appropriateness of the time of the advent has often been pointed out. The Jewish world was expectant of the coming of the Messiah. The Roman world, in its rapid spread, had contributed a measure of peace and security, which had been previously unparalleled. It had, moreover, developed communications to a remarkable extent, linking all the strategic centers of the empire with Rome. The Greek language was widely used for trade and communication and supplied an admirable medium for the transmission of the gospel. But it may be questioned how much of these advantages were in Paul's mind when he wrote this statement, however valuable they may be. In the context it is clear that his thought is still centered on servitude to the law and the most reasonable assumption, therefore, is to regard the *fullness* as the limit of God's testing time under the law, during which the hopelessness of man's servitude was fully demonstrated. Paul is convinced, as the early Christians were generally, that the coming of Christ was not by accident but by divine appointment"[2]

B. BORN OF A WOMAN, BORN UNDER THE LAW

While Christ was divine His humanity came from His mother. His humanity was essential in order to be "under the law" and to fulfill its requirement in our behalf.

C. IN ORDER THAT WE MIGHT BE REDEEMED AND ADOPTED
1. **Redeemed**. Once again the term *redeem* carries the idea of setting slaves free from their bondage by paying a price. There were millions of slaves in the Roman empire at this time. The right price could purchase a slave to be kept or freed. Paul's idea is that Christ paid the price for our redemption and freed us from the bondage of sin and death. This term strengthens the idea that we are now free men - freed for freedom!
2. **Adopted as sons**. Greek and Roman laws were well acquainted with the institution of adoption. Those who were not natural heirs could acquire the status of natural sonship. The newly adopted son was legally in every respect on a level with those born into that family.
D. SONS RECEIVE THE INDWELLING SPIRIT

As adopted members of the divine family of God, we receive the same Spirit by which Jesus so intimately addressed God as "Abba, Father" (Mark 14:36). The retention of the Aramaic term *Abba* for Greek speaking peoples is unusual. Perhaps it is due to the fact that Jesus Himself used it so in the hour of His greatest earthly need when He besought the Father just prior to His death. It has been suggested that the term held an especially intimate meaning for Christ, and for that reason the church held it as sacred. *Abba* was also a domestic term by which the father in the Hebrew patriarchy was called in the affectionate intimacy of the family circle. One story has it that only the firstborn son was allowed to call the father of the Hebrew patriarchy "Abba." It was among the greatest expectations of a Hebrew father that the first word his firstborn son would utter would be addressed to him and that word would be *Abba*. The point is the intimacy of our new relationship with God.

We do not receive the Spirit to make us sons. Paul says it is because we are sons that we receive the Spirit of Christ. Not all men are sons of God. We must be born again into the divine family. Then it becomes ours as sons to receive from the Father the indwelling gift of the Holy Spirit. It is by the Holy Spirit that we have the privilege of intimately addressing God as, "Abba, Father," with the same intimacy that Jesus Himself has with the Father. As our interceder (Romans 8:26, 27) the Holy Spirit cries, "Abba, Father," when we cry, "Abba, Father" (Romans 8:15; Galatians 4:6). Such intimacy of sonship in the divine family could not be achieved by the law of Moses. Only through Christ, and by faith in Him, could this inexpressible family privilege be obtained in our behalf.

III. Law Makes Us Slaves Again, 4:8-11

However at that time, when you did not know God, you were slaves to those which by nature are no gods. But now that you have come to know God, or rather to be known by God, how is it that you turn back again to the weak and worthless elemental things, to which you desire to be enslaved all over again? You observe days and months and seasons and years. I fear for you, that perhaps I have labored over you in vain (Galatians 4:8-11).

With these words, "However, at that time...But now," Paul sets up a great contrast between the Galatians' former status as slaves to sin under idolatry, their present status as men free from sin now that they know the true God, and their future status of returning to the bondage of sin if they accept the law of Moses for salvation. Paul uses this same language in the Ephesian letter to set up the contrast between their former status as pagans when they were "far off" from God, and their present status "in Christ" of being "near" to God because of Christ's blood (Ephesians 2:11-13).

A. THE GALATIANS' PAST STATUS - "at that time"

The words "at that time" describe the Galatians' past status in idolatry prior to Paul and Barnabas preaching the gospel in the Galatian regions (Acts chs.13-14).

1. **When you did not know God**. As pagans, the Galatians had no knowledge of the one true God. An example of their idolatry at Lystra, after Paul healed a lame man, has them attempting to worship Barnabas and Paul as the gods Zeus and Hermes (Acts 14:8-18).

2. **Were slaves to no gods**. That is, slaves to idols that are not gods, to idolatrous ritual that had no power to free them from their bondage to sin.

a. **No gods**. Both the prophets (Jeremiah 2:11; 5:7; 16:20) and Paul (Acts 19:26) seek to convey by the term *no gods* that idols are nonrealities. They are by their nature wood, stone, marble, not gods at all. They represent nothing of substance reality (cf. Acts 14:15; 1 Corinthians 8:4; 12:2). The worship of such, however elaborate and sincere, is absolutely vain. Gods other than the one true God simply do not exist to reciprocate.

b. **Their hopeless condition**. This is graphically depicted in Paul's Ephesian letter (Ephesians 2:11-22), which applies equally to the Galatians. They were
   (1) separate from Christ
   (2) excluded from the commonwealth of Israel
   (3) strangers to the covenants of promise
   (4) far off
   (5) aliens
   (6) having no hope
   (7) without God in the world

B. THE GALATIANS' PRESENT STATUS - *"But now"*
   1. **You have come to know God**. They had come to know God through the preaching of the gospel. Paul, in his first sermon to the Galatians at Pisidian Antioch (Acts 13:16-41), referred to God nine times and in reference to God used the personal singular pronoun *He* twelve times. The singularity and unity of the one true God is emphasized.

      Paul uses two different words to distinguish between the knowledge of God they did not have while in idolatry (Galatians 4:8) and their knowledge of God they now have as Christians (Galatians 4:9). As pagans they knew not God even factually. But now they know God experientially and personally.

      Jesus uses a form of this last word to say that to know God in this way is to have eternal life (John 17:3).

   2. **Or rather to be known by God**. Here is another distinction between having a factual knowledge of God and God knowing us intimately as His sons, as members of His divine family.

God has knowledge of all men and of all things relating to all men at all times (Luke 12:7). But there is that sense in which God does not know men who are not His family members (cf. Matthew 7:22, 23).

C. THE GALATIANS' FUTURE STATUS UNDER LAW - "*To be enslaved all over again*"

1. **A return to slavery**. The Gentile Galatians were never under the law to return to it. But if they accepted the law, they would return "again" to the same kind of slavery they experienced in the idolatrous rituals of their former paganism that could not free them from their sins. If they accepted the law of Moses as essential to salvation, they would espouse "the weak and worthless elemental things" of that law that could no more free them from their future sins than could the rituals of their former idol worship. This is tantamount to saying that the law of Moses, or any such legal system (e.g. Catholicism, Hinduism, Islam), or the perversion of Christianity into a legalistic keeping of Christ's commandments, will turn sons of God and heirs of eternal life back into bond-slaves to sin and death.

   Paul is implying that the works of the law of Moses, which he labels as "weak and worthless elemental things," are as impotent and worthless to free us from our sins as the weak and worthless elements of pagan idolatry.

2. **A return to vanity**. The Galatians' observance of Jewish "days [sabbaths] and months [new moons] and seasons [recurrent festivals] and years" [jubilee years] is classified as "vain." Though given by God for the benefit of men, the ordinances of the law are powerless to remove our future sins. The acceptance of any legal system, which necessarily displaces faith in Christ, is a return to vanity and consequently a return to the bondage of our future sins.

   CONCLUSION: Like Jewish ritual and pagan idolatry, no traditional accretions of men today have the power to remove sin and its curse. Only Christ through the gospel has that power. Christ alone in His atoning sacrifice redeemed us from the curse of law and the penalty of sin and death. Only by faith in Him can we become heirs of the divine estate, members of the divine family, and receive the Spirit of our adoption enabling us to have intimate conversations with the Father.

When Christians today place their trust in any person or system other than Christ Himself, they return to the same weak and worthless rudiments that were powerless to make us right with God before we became Christians. This will result in a return to bondage issuing from our future sins from which there is no remission outside of Christ.

Spiritual Probing
Chapter Eight

1. Why does Paul in Galatians 4:1-3 relate to these Gentiles Christians the spiritual condition of the Jews when they were under the law of Moses?

2. Paul says that when the Jews were under the law they "were held in bondage to the elemental things of the world." What do you think these elemental things are? If you believe these elemental things are Jewish rituals which Paul mentions in Galatians 4:10, days, months, seasons, and years of the Jewish law system, do you believe that this bondage was to the observance of these rituals, or that it was bondage to sin from which these "weak and worthless elemental things" could not set one free?

3. Paul uses the words bondage and freedom antithetically (Galatians 2:4; 5:1). If freedom is from sin, to what were the Galatians in bondage before Paul preached to them? Were the Galatian Gentiles, before Paul came with the gospel, ever under the law of Moses? To what were they held in bondage when Paul first came to them (Galatians 4:8)? Merely to idols, or also to sin?

4. According to Galatians 4:9, those early Christians would have returned to bondage if they had accepted the teaching of the Judaizers. Since they were never under the law to have returned to the law, what is the bondage to which they would have returned?

5. Does the Galatian letter teach by principle that a justified person can return to the bondage of sin and death by attempting to live under a legal system of law? What will happen to one of God's sons who views the works of faith as meritorious works of legal law? Does that view exist today? How have you observed it expressing itself?

6. If a Christian cannot so misplace his faith away from Christ to the point of losing his salvation, why did Paul say that he feared that he may well have labored in vain to bring the gospel to the Galatians (Galatians 4:11)?

Chapter Nine
A Contrast of Affections and Motives
Galatians 4:12-20

Of all of his letters, this section is perhaps the most emotional and touching of Paul's verbal outpourings to his children in the faith. We know that Paul's great Christian heart was touched by the Corinthians as a caring father who spiritually begat them in Christ (1 Corinthians 4:15), and again by the Thessalonians for whom he tenderly cared like a nursing mother (1 Thessalonians 2:7). But in this letter to the Galatians Paul feels the distance that now separates them from him, not to mention from Christ, to the extent of such perplexity as to just how to handle the situation. In his attempt to close the gap between them he reveals a painful anxiety that grips him like a woman's birth pains.

I beg of you, brethren, become as I am, for I also have become as you are. You have done me no wrong; but you know that it was because of a bodily illness that I preached the gospel to you the first time; and that which was a trial to you in my bodily condition you did not despise or loathe, but you received me as an angel of God, as Christ Jesus Himself. Where then is that sense of blessing you had? For I bear you witness that, if possible, you would have plucked out your eyes and given them to me. So have I become your enemy by telling you the truth? They eagerly seek you, not commendably, but they wish to shut you out, so that you will seek them. But it is good always to be eagerly sought in a commendable manner, and not only when I am present with you. My children, with whom I am again in labor until Christ is formed in you - but I could wish to be present with you now and to change my tone, for I am perplexed about you (Galatians 4:12-20).

The Galatians were fickle. Ramsay observes that "the Galatians were intellectually quick enough. The 'folly' with which they are charged (Galatians 3:1) arose not from obtuseness but from fickleness and levity."[1] R.C. Bell's quotation of Julius Caesar's characterization of the Gauls is revealing: "The infirmity of the Gauls is that they are fickle in their resolves, fond of change, and not to be trusted."[2] An example of this is the Galatian flip-flop at Lystra, where, when they first heard Paul speak, they attempted to worship him as a god, but soon afterward they were urged on by Jews from Antioch and Iconium who won over the Lystrians and stoned Paul and left him for dead (Acts 14:8-19). So this manifestation of their fickle character is not surprising, but it is frustrating. If it is asked, then, what is the point of this address by which Paul intends to bring the Galatians back into freedom's fold, it has been suggested that it may well have no such point. It may be but a compulsive extension of the same cry of frustration that burst forth earlier when he said, "You foolish Galatians, who has bewitched you, before whose eyes Jesus Christ was publicly portrayed as crucified?" (3:1).

On the other hand we should remember that the line of defense exposes the line of attack. Perhaps there is something of a defense here against the Judaizers' attempt to assassinate Paul's character. When Paul reminds the Galatians that he preached the gospel to them due to some physical malady, and then writes that "it is good always to be eagerly sought in a commendable manner, and not only when I am present with you," could this be a defense against an attack on his character, that he had preached the gospel to them for personal reasons rather than for their eternal benefit? Perhaps Paul, in addition to revealing his throbbing heart, is defending his sincere motives for preaching the gospel to them in the first place, and even for writing to them in such pungent terms.

I. A Special Plea to the Galatians, 4:12,13

Had the false teachers accused Paul of preaching to the Galatians out of some motive other than genuine concern for their souls? Had he been accused of exploiting them to aggrandize himself? It seems conclusive from one of his opening statements (1:10) that he was accused of using flattery to gain the Galatians' confidence. Not only, then, had the Judaizers attacked

Paul's apostleship and his gospel, but his character as well. He responds in the form of a plea.

A. IDENTIFY WITH ME EVEN AS I IDENTIFY WITH YOU

As a Christian whose confidence for salvation is now totally in Christ, Paul identifies more with the Galatian Gentiles than with Jews. On this ground he pleads, "become as I am, for I also have become as you are." That is, a once proud Jew whose confidence was in the law and in his flesh to be right with God, but now, as they, Gentiles, he stands on no grounds but Christ and Him crucified. Such a radical change of ground and such consistency of life offers evidence of the genuineness of his position.

B. REMEMBER THE REASON I PREACHED THE GOSPEL TO YOU IN THE FIRST PLACE

Could Paul have made a geographical change of evangelistic plans? He reminds them of what they knew, that the real reason for choosing the Galatian province was due to a bodily affliction. It seems that Paul's original evangelistic course did not include the route from Pisidian Antioch to Derbe, but that either he was stricken with some malady, or that some recurrence of a pre-existing affliction caused him to select the Galatian province as an alternative to his original plans. William Ramsay suggests that Paul could have been afflicted with a fever, perhaps due to malaria, that was intermittent, and that the recurrence caused him to change his course to the higher altitudes of Pisidian Antioch.[3]

C. REMEMBER HOW EAGERLY YOU RECEIVED ME

Whatever the reason for the change of geography, it turned out to the Galatians' salvation. They accepted Paul and the gospel eagerly, which seems to be the meaning of, "You have done me no wrong." Their reception of Paul and his message was so enthusiastic that they treated him, in spite of his bodily appearance, as an angel of the Lord (reflecting their reception of his message, as an angel is a divine messenger), even as Jesus Himself (reflecting their reception of his person).

II. The Galatians' Feelings For Paul, 4:12-16

A. FORMERLY, 4:12-16

When Paul first preached the gospel to them, the Galatians' response was commendable as well as enthusiastic.

1. **They neither despised nor loathed him**. Their response was not one of revulsion at his bodily illness, which was physically obvious. Nor did they "spit out" when they saw him, a literal translation of "you despised not." The idea of the evil eye was wide spread in antiquity that a sickly or diseased person could spread his contagion by looking at those who observed him. "One way to ward off this harmful effect was by spitting...spitting was a regular part of the social conventions associated with the ideas about the evil eye....Theocritus as early as the third century B.C. said that one could ward off the evil eye by spitting three times."[4] Ridderbos explains, "Illness, physical infirmity, and adversity were regarded even by the Jews, as representing the opposition and penalty of the deity, but more so by the Gentiles (cf. Acts 28:4)."[5]

2. **Received him as an angel, as Jesus Christ**. The Galatians received Paul, not as one who contaminated by the evil eye, but "as an angel of God, as Christ Jesus Himself." While *angelos* can be translated "angel," where twice already used is its clear meaning (Galatians 1:8; 3:19), it can also mean "messenger." This may recall the incident at Lystra, one of the cities of south Galatia, where Paul healed a cripple and the citizens began to view Paul and Barnabas as gods who came down in the likeness of men (Acts 14:8-18). The connection here is about pagan conceptions of gods visiting the earth in the form of men, and, as Witherington informs us, "were likely to come incognito, sometimes so disguised that they would be quite unrecognizable. They would come as a feeble old man or as a sickly woman...in order to test those that they ruled to see what kind of persons they really were."[6] When this is coupled with the miraculous signs that Paul worked in their midst (Acts 14:8-11; Galatians 3:5) it is easy to understand how these pagans

could have viewed Paul as Hermes in disguise - the messenger of the gods.

3. **They would have given Paul their own eyes**. Some commentators have said that Paul's, "you would have plucked out your eyes and given them to me," was a proverbial saying. But Donald Guthrie replies, "There is, however, no evidence that this was a proverbial saying," and the meaning of the statement to be preferred is that Paul did indeed have an eye disease of some kind, and that the Galatians' gratitude for the gospel was such that, if they could, they would literally have given him their own eyes."[7] Paul's, "See with what *large* letters I am writing to you with my own hand" (6:11), evokes a worthy question: "If we ask what sort of person needs 'large print editions' and often writes with large characters the answer is a person with a visual impairment." [8] Thus, though his impairment was physically unattractive, due to his miracles, which confirmed him as an apostolic spokesman for God, and the power of the gospel message, the Galatians did him no wrong by revolting against him, but rather received him as the very messenger of the Lord himself. By this means Paul is reminding them of the joyous gratitude the gospel first excited in them.

B. PRESENTLY, 4:16

Originally, after Paul had preached the gospel to them "the first time," on that first missionary journey, the Galatians' feelings towards Paul were one of deep gratitude born of the gospel that brought them out of empty idolatry into eternal life. But now the atmosphere has changed. Paul senses it, and either asks, "So have I become your enemy by telling you the truth?" or, he exclaims, "So, now I have become your enemy by telling you the truth!" In either translation it assumes he knows something of their present change of attitude toward him. Is such a response in answer to the information conveyed to him by whatever source originally informed him of their recent change of belief and consequent change of attitude towards him? Whatever the source Paul now knows that they regard him with far less appreciation and confidence than when he preached the gospel to them the first time. Was it due to further indictments made by Paul's detractors, this time against his character, that his motives for preaching the gospel to them were viewed as less than for a genuine desire for their salvation? If Paul means that their present view is due to a new view of the gospel as interpreted by the Judaizers, and due to their present view of his authority as less than apostolic, then his "So, I am now your enemy for having told you the truth!" refers to when he originally preached the truth of the gospel to them. This stands in strong contrast to their original view of him as a spokesman from God, and the view they now have is the result of the message taught them by those of the circumcision.

III. A Contrast of Motives for Pursuing the Galatians' Confidence, 4:17, 18

A. THE JUDAIZERS' MOTIVES

The Judaizers were eagerly courting the Galatians' confidence. Paul responds that to be sought after in a commendable manner for a commendable matter is good, but that the Judaizers would manipulate the Galatians by persuading them to think they were not yet saved. Paul says, "they wish to shut you out," that is, from salvation, "so that you will seek them," that is, their message, and fellowship with those of the circumcision.

B. PAUL'S MOTIVES

He had brought the Galatians salvation, confidence, joy, and hope. He had preached good news of redemption to former pagans whose idolatrous practice could not free them from their bondage to sin. He confirmed his message by signs following. Would such confirmation from God be used to endorse a false teacher?

IV. Paul's Parental Affection For Them, 4:19, 20

His true feeling for the Galatians was like a parent whose heart breaks for a child who chooses the path of destruction. He had begotten them in the gospel, and now he is in emotional labor over them again: (1) He addresses them as a parent. He pleads with them as "my children." (2) He hurts for them as a woman about to be delivered of her baby, "I am again in labor until Christ be formed in you." (3) He wishes he could do more than write a letter to them. The "tone" of the letter was abrupt, candid, terse, defensive, and indicting. How else could he convey the seriousness of their defection? Yet, his parent's heart would prefer to be present, as he says, "and to change my tone," to let them hear the tone of voice that conveyed the deep feeling of concern and genuine love he has for them. (4) He is in a quandary as to how to handle the matter at Galatia. "I am perplexed about you."

CONCLUSION: Had Paul, the great psychologist, knowing both human nature and the nature of these Galatians, judged correctly that they would take exception to the cutting edges of his letter thus far? Did he then in anticipation of their emotions ruling over their reason make this loving attempt to persuade them that, while such stringent measures were necessary, they were said from a loving heart that was drenched in tears and frustrated with perplexity? In the same spirit with which he sought to strengthen the Ephesians by "speaking the truth in love," he wrote this statement to his children in the Lord at Galatia. They were fickle, but they were also babes in Christ. And a loving parent uses every means at his disposal to correct an unthinking and wayward child.

Spiritual Probing
Chapter Nine

1. Why do you suppose Paul wrote this particular section of the letter? Was it merely a compulsive outcry? Or do you think it was a defense of his motives for seeking out the Galatians that the false teachers had misrepresented? Or could it have been both?
2. What do you suppose Paul meant by saying, "Become as I am, for I also have become as you are"?
3. I think, in the light of Galatians 4:15 and 6:11, Paul's "bodily illness" produced poor eyesight. Is that a reasonable consideration? If not, why did Paul write the epistle, or at least the unprecedented and long closing statement, in such oversized characters?
4. Do you suppose that Paul's "perplexity" of spirit over the Galatian situation may have caused him to write with such candor that he felt the need at this point to confirm his genuine love and affection for them?

Chapter Ten
The Allegory of Hagar and Sarah
Galatians 4:21-31

Paul's allegory is his capstone argument concluding his appeal to the authority of Old Testament Scripture in a final attempt to clarify the basic error of legalism and the truth of the gospel.

The question is, why does Paul employ an allegory? It seems very likely that the Judaizers did. Once again we see the need to interpret a bit of Galatians as we would a telephone conversation of which we hear only one side. They could have reasoned with the Galatians as follows: Even as Abraham married Sarah, so God entered into a marriage covenant with Israel. Even as Isaac, born of that union, was born free, so those under the law are the only ones that are free. Since Gentiles are not under the law, they are slaves and must come under the law to be free. So Paul responds with an allegory of his own. He does this with two goals in mind: (1) to demonstrate that a correct allegorizing of the historical facts of Scripture demonstrates that the law produces bondage, not freedom from sin, and (2) to expose the fallacy of the Judaizers' allegory.

There are three stages in Paul's reasoning. The first is historical, recalling the facts as recorded in Genesis (Galatians 4:21-23). The second is allegorical, presenting the spiritual truths that are by nature resident in the facts (Galatians 4:24-27). The third is the application to legalists and to Christians (Galatians 4:28-31).

I. History: The Facts Recorded in Scripture, 4:21-23

Tell me, you who want to be under law, do you not listen to the law? For it is written that Abraham had two sons, one by the bondwoman and one by the free woman. But the son by the bondwoman was born according to the flesh, and the son by the free woman through the promise (Galatians 4:21-23).

Did the Galatians want to be under the law? It appears so. Paul has just said that they "desire to be enslaved all over again." This time it would be to the elemental things of the law (Galatians 4:9). That being true he bases his message on the authority of Scripture: "you who want to be under law, do you not listen to the law?" Had the Judaizers left something out? Were there other facts to be considered in the allegory? Paul seems to be saying, Get the whole story first. "For it is written..." (in Genesis 16, 17, and 21).

A. ABRAHAM HAD TWO SONS

It seems the emphasis should be on the word *two*, "Abraham had *two* sons," as if Paul's opponents had spoken only of Isaac. A perceptive person would see that this fact alone, that Abraham had two sons and that only one of them was the father of the Jews, would actually neutralize the Judaizers' argumentation that one either had to be a Jew or accept the Jewish religion to be blessed. The Jew placed much value on being Abraham's fleshly descendant, as if that biological relationship guaranteed salvation. Could not the Jews argue from Genesis 12:3 and 22:18 that God had promised the redemptive blessing to Abraham's seed, and that therefore, the Gentiles should imitate the Jews to the point of circumcision and keeping the law? (Hence, Paul's argument on the singularity, rather than the plurality, of that seed promise in Galatians 3:16). But such boasting fails to remember that Abraham had two sons, Ishmael by Hagar as well as Isaac by Sarah. Someone has observed, if physical descent from Abraham is so all-important, then Jews are no better off than Ishmaelites. Good point.

B. ISAAC BY SARAH AND ISHMAEL BY HAGAR

There is a distinct difference between Isaac and Ishmael, even as between their mothers Hagar and Sarah, and that difference is significant to the allegory and its application.

C. A BASIC DIFFERENCE BETWEEN THESE MOTHERS AND THEIR SONS

1. **The difference between Hagar and Sarah and their sons**. Hagar was a slave woman, and as such her offspring would

have been born into slavery. It appears the Judaizers, if indeed they employed the allegory, had appealed only to Sarah and to her freeborn son Isaac. But the fact of this second son, a historical fact to be reckoned with, requires a revision of their allegory. To what would these women and their sons correctly correspond in Judaism and Christianity?

2. **The difference in the birth of their sons**. Whereas Ishmael was born "according to the flesh," that is, the natural way, Isaac was born "through the promise," by means of divine intervention. Isaac's birth required God's special attention.

II. Allegory: Other Truths To Which the Facts Correspond, 4:24-27

An allegory is a true story with another meaning corresponding to the nature of the facts. It is more than an illustration. Paul uses it to teach the truth. Paul's allegory, as he writes by the Spirit's guidance, presents a real spiritual truth that is embodied in the nature of those actual historical events.

The facts must be correctly allegorized. The facts in the story correspond to other truths of like nature. What truths in the law and in the gospel correspond to these historical facts? Paul answers

This is allegorically speaking, for these women are two covenants: one proceeding from Mount Sinai bearing children who are to be slaves; she is Hagar. Now this Hagar is Mount Sinai in Arabia, and corresponds to the present Jerusalem, for she is in slavery with her children. But the Jerusalem above is free; she is our mother. For it is written, "Rejoice, barren woman who does not bear; Break forth and shout, you who are not in labor; For more numerous are the children of the desolate than of the one who has a husband" (Galatians 4:24-27).

A. VIEWING THE FACTS AND THE TRUTHS TO WHICH THEY CORRESPOND

The word *correspond* (Galatians 4:25), used in a military sense, means to be in line with, or to be in the same row with, as soldiers in a file. The idea is to answer to or to be in the same category with. The facts and events in the story correspond in nature with other truths, as when Paul says, "these women are two covenants." Both

Sarah and Hagar correspond in nature to the nature of the old and new covenants. One, a slave woman, bears children into slavery. She corresponds to the old covenant that condemns and holds sinners in bondage. Sarah, a free woman, bears children into freedom. She corresponds to the new covenant that frees sinners from their bondage. We may better understand the allegory by aligning, or paralleling, these two women with the truths to which they correspond as Paul gives them to us.

B. THE ALLEGORY MUST CORRECTLY REPRESENT THE FACTS COMMENSURATE WITH THEIR TRUE HISTORICAL NATURE

1. **Sarah the free woman corresponds to the new covenant**. Neither Sarah nor Isaac could possibly correspond to the covenant that enslaves men to their sins. The old covenant as a legal system could make no one free from sin. It could only bring men into bondage. The law therefore by its very nature could not possibly be a true spiritual parallel to Sarah or to her freeborn son Isaac. To allegorize Sarah and Isaac as correspondents to freedom under the law would be a contradiction of the nature of the law. But Sarah, as a free woman giving birth to a free son, corresponds to the new covenant given for freedom from sin. Understanding this would expose the error of the Judaizers' allegory.

2. **Hagar the slave woman corresponds to the old covenant**. The law - the old covenant - is a perfect spiritual parallel to Hagar the bondwoman and her slave-born son Ishmael inasmuch as it holds men in slavery to sin and death.

3. **Hagar corresponds to Mount Sinai in Arabia**. The following quotation from Lenski is an able exposition of Paul's meaning:

   "This is not a trivial geographical remark but a significant statement. Arabia includes the Sinaitic peninsula. Hagar went south to Beersheba, and Ishmael dwelt in Paran, the territory near Sinai. Sinai is thus connected with Hagar's son and his descendants, and Arabia, in which Sinai is located is not connected with the promise as all Bible readers know. Not in the promised land but in the Arabian desert, which separated Israel from Canaan when it was at Sinai, was the law given. This law was thus not the fulfillment of the promise given to Abraham. The very place where the law was given, Arabia, Sinai, connected it with the slave woman Hagar and with her son Ishmael, born 'to slavery.' Paul's statement that Sinai lies in Arabia thus justifies the identification of Hagar with Sinai, with the law and slavery."[1]

4. **Hagar corresponds to the present Jerusalem in slavery with her children.** Jerusalem figuratively parallels Hagar and Ishmael inasmuch as it was the center of Judaism and legalism. All non-Christian inhabitants, which constituted the greater part of the population, were in bondage to sin under the law.

C. JERUSALEM ABOVE IS FREE

Hagar the bondwoman	Sarah the free woman
Corresponds to:	Corresponds to:
The Old Covenant bearing slave children (like Ishmael)	The New Covenant bearing free children (like Isaac)
Earthly Jerusalem in bondage	Heavenly Jerusalem - free
Not sharing the inheritance	Sharing the inheritance

Paul quotes Isaiah 54:1 where the prophet sees Jerusalem desolated in Babylonian captivity. Sarah answers to Jerusalem's condition in captivity where she was "desolate," being without children. But Isaiah sees Jerusalem set free from captivity to return to her land where she will multiply greatly and serve her purpose to bring in the Messiah. The point of the prophecy, it seems, is to give courage to Israel when in captivity in a foreign land she would think herself as hopeless without a national future. This would be the natural outlook for any nation in antiquity that would be relocated geographically as was Israel and Judah in the captivities to Assyria and Babylonia. In another land, in another culture with another language their children could be expected to forget their own national history, and to absorb the idolatrous culture and language of their captors. Such conditions could anticipate the entire dissolution and loss of the identity of the nation of Israel. But the prophet foresees the preservation of Israel in captivity, a return to her homeland, and a divine purpose for the future to bring in the Messiah. Paul's point in appealing to this word from Isaiah, it seems, is to claim the fulfillment of the prophecy that Jerusalem's future would experience a greater number of spiritual children born to Sarah through Isaac than were born to Hagar. This Jerusalem, which Isaiah foresaw and to which Sarah corresponds, is our mother, says Paul. This is the heavenly Jerusalem (Hebrews 12:22, 23; Revelation 3:12; 21:2), the church of Christ, set free from the bondage of sin. She stands in contrast to those in bondage to sin under the law.

III. Application: To Christians and To Those Under Law, 4:28-31

And you brethren, like Isaac, are children of promise. But as at that time he who was born according to the flesh persecuted him who was born according to the Spirit, so it is now also. But what does the Scripture say? "Cast out the bondwoman and her son, for the son of the bondwoman shall not be an heir with the son of the free woman." So then, brethren, we are not children of a bondwoman, but of the free woman (Galatians 4:28-31).

   A. THE NATURAL CORRESPONDENCE BETWEEN PERSONS IN THE ALLIGORY

      1. **Isaac and Christians**, 4:28. Like Isaac, Christians are children of promise. Both of the promises God made to Abraham, the seed promise and Isaac's birth, were fulfilled by God's supernatural intervention. Without God's intervention into the biology of Abraham and Sarah, Isaac could not have been born as promised. Without God's supernatural intervention into history,

by means of a virgin conception and by means of the death and resurrection of Christ, we could not be saved from sin. The natural parallels are obvious.

2. **Ishmael and Isaac and legalists and Christians**, 4:29. Paul's "at that time...so it is now also," expresses the natural correspondence between Ishmael and Isaac and legalists and Christians: those who live according to the flesh persecute those who live by the Spirit.

B. THE AUTHORITY OF SCRIPTURE, 4:30

As surely as God told Abraham to listen to Sarah and to cast out the bondwoman and her son (21:10, 12), we are to remove all legalism from the body of Christ.

CONCLUSION: "So then, brethren, we are not children of a bondwoman, but of the free woman." "So then" is a statement of conclusion. The facts in the matter, the allegory, and the application all considered, we must conclude that God's new family members are not bond-slaves to either the old covenant or to any law system like it.

Spiritual Probing
Chapter Ten

1. Paul probably used an allegory because the Judaizers did. Whom do you think the Judaizers might have used in their allegory? How could they have allegorized Sarah and Isaac? Hagar and Ishmael?

2. Do you agree that the Judaistic emphasis on being a physical descendant of Abraham in order to inherit the promised blessing would have been offset by Paul's reminder that Abraham had two sons, one that came by the Spirit? What argument could the Judaizers have made by allegorizing only from Isaac? How does the fact that Abraham had two sons offset that reasoning?

3. What does it mean, "The Jerusalem above is free; she is our mother"?

4. What truths in the law and the gospel correctly correspond to Hagar and Ishmael, and to Sarah and Isaac? Who corresponds to bondage? Why? Who corresponds to freedom? Why?

5. Paul's great point in the allegory is that God casts out the legal means of earning justification and freely bestows it on Abraham's seed by faith. Of course, we should cast out legalism. Do you think we are obligated to cast out legalists who view the law of faith as a legal system? Does Paul's, "A little leaven leavens the whole lump of dough" (Galatians 5:9) apply here?

PART THREE: PRACTICAL ARGUMENT
Galatians 5:1-6:18

Consequences of Legalism Upon Our Freedom
Galatians 5:1-12

It was for freedom that Christ set us free; therefore keep standing firm and do not be subject again to a yoke of slavery (Galatians 5:1).

This statement fits well as a conclusion to the allegory. That may well be what Paul had in mind for it. But as the letter is now divided it appears to serve as a statement of transition from the allegory to the apostle's exhortation to stand fast in our Christian freedom, and so introduces the final division of the letter, The Practical Argument.

A STATEMENT OF TRANSITION

With these opening words, Paul makes a distinct transition from argument to application. Chapters 1 through 4 are written in the indicative mood wherein Paul reasons, argues, and concludes. He battles theologically to expose the error of legalism and to sustain the truth of the gospel. But in this last section of the letter there is a distinct change of content and thrust. Chapters 5 and 6 are written in the imperative mood. Paul now gives commands and urges directives. He asks for a response. In these closing chapters he makes a transition from theology to practical application. He uses verbs such as *be, wait, walk, work, love, live, do,* and *do not.*

The transition is highlighted in chapter 5 in the parallel verses 1 and 13. The first clause of each of these verses sums up the content of chapters 1 through 4, which is written in the indicative mood. Notice in verse 1a, "It was for freedom that Christ set us free," then in verse 13a, "For you were called to freedom, brethren." But the last clause of each of these verses sums up the imperative content of these final chapters. Notice verse 1b, "therefore keep standing firm and do not be subject again to a yoke of slavery." Then in verse 13b, "only do not turn your freedom into an opportunity for the flesh, but through love serve one another." It is also noteworthy that the last clause of each of these verses is couched in imperative statements that are both positive and negative. Notice 5:1, first a positive imperative, "keep standing firm," then follows a negative imperative, "and do not be subject again to a yoke of slavery." Then in verse 13 Paul reverses the polarity: first a negative imperative, "do not turn your freedom into an opportunity for the flesh," then a positive imperative, "but through love serve one another." What emerges is the literary balance in Paul's background as an accomplished rhetorician.

This literary balance can be set out in the following form:

The First Clause of each verse sums up the Indicative Argumentation:
   It was for freedom that Christ set us free, 5:1a.
   For you were called for freedom, brethren, 5:13a.
The Last Clause of each verse sums up the Imperative Argumentation:
   therefore keep standing firm and do not be subject again to a yoke of bondage, 5:1b.
   only do not turn your freedom into an opportunity for the flesh, but through love serve one another, 5:13b.
The Imperative Statements of both verses are positive and negative:
   Positive imperative: Keep standing firm, 5:1a.
   Negative imperative: do not be subject again to a yoke of slavery, 5:1b.
   Negative imperative: only do not turn your freedom into an opportunity for the flesh, 5:13a.
   Positive imperative: but through love serve one another, 5:13b.

Paul's point seems to be that while Christ freed us from the deadly curse of the law, it becomes our responsibility to obediently cooperate with Him to maintain that freedom. Mere intellectual belief is not enough. We must trust and obey.

In this lesson Paul not only exhorts the Galatians to stand fast in their Christian freedom but to recognize and take caution against the consequences of legalism.

I.   The Apostle's Manifesto, 5:1

Paul's great declaration of the result of Christ's work is the believer's freedom and Christ's intent for him to remain free. Christ actually set us free from sin for continual freedom from sin.

A.   CHRISTIANS ARE FREED FOR FREEDOM

We have not been set free only to return to our former slavery. Our Father wants us to remain free. But the question rises, What is the slavery from which we are set free? And what is the freedom for which we are freed? Is this freedom from the law or from sin? If we say Paul meant that we are freed from sin to remain free from sin, then, inasmuch as Paul also said, "do not be subject again to a yoke of slavery," we must affirm that the Christian can be subject again to the slavery of sin. This means that the Christian can so sin as to lose his precious salvation, a position heartily denied by many evangelicals - not to say by most believers. Since this view sets up tension with the theology of the impossibility of apostasy, those who maintain that theology consistently interpret the passage to teach that Paul meant that the Galatians were not to return to the ritual drudgery of the law's ordinances. Let us consider whether Paul means freedom from sin or freedom from law.

1.   **Freed from the law of Moses**? Though some Jews at Iconium believed the gospel (Acts 14:1), Paul addresses the Galatian letter as if the recipients were Gentiles. He writes as if all the Galatians were at one time in idolatry having no knowledge of the one true God: "However at that time, when you did not know God, you were slaves to those which by nature are no gods" (4:8). This could hardly apply to Jews who had been virtually cured of idolatry through their captivity centuries earlier. The churches of Galatia were predominantly Gentile. This becomes significant as we take knowledge of the fact that the Gentile Christians at Galatia were never under the law of

Moses to have been freed from it. They therefore could not have returned to it, as Paul says, "again." If they placed themselves under the law it would not be a return to it. It would be their initial submission to it. From what, then, did Christ set them free? What is the bondage to which they could "again" be yoked? The bondage to which they would return? And in what way could they be yoked to that bondage?

2. **Freed from the curse of the law**. The wages of sin is death, and since all have sinned all have come under the curse of death (Romans 6:23; 3:23). The law pronounced the curse of sin and death upon the entire human race whether under the law or not (Galatians 3:13, 22; Romans 3:19). The purpose of the law was to educate all men to the fatality of their sin and to the curse of death pronounced by that law. Consequently Gentiles, though not under the law of Moses, committed sin and were indicted by the curse of the law. When the Galatians were justified they were set free from the curse of the law.

3. **Freed from sin to be free from sin**. When our faith is reckoned for righteousness we are set free from more than our past sins. We are set free from the law's curse of our future sins. Paul reasons in the Roman letter that there is no condemnation to those who are in Christ inasmuch as by the cross and by the law of the Spirit of life He has made us free from the law of sin and death (the law that separates us from God when we sin). Rather than our sin condemning us, He now condemns our sin (Romans 8:1-3). The glorious truth is that by faith in Christ sinners are set free from the bondage to past sins and kept free from bondage to our future sins.

This truth also emerges in Romans chapter 6. The Romans knew that they had been freed from sin for freedom from future sin. Paul's "Or do you not know" does not express an ignorance on the part of the Roman Christians relating to what happened to them at their baptism. His question is rhetorical. It carries an affirmative answer in it that is understood by the Romans. He then proceeds to build an argument for Christian living on what they knew. It was precisely on the grounds that the Romans knew that at baptism they were freed for freedom that some in the church falsely claimed that freedom from sin liberates us to a life of sin without restraint. They even claimed on the grounds of freedom from sin that we should engage in sin that grace might increase! Paul's rhetorical question makes this clear, "What shall we say then? Are we to continue in sin so that grace might increase?" (Romans 6:1). The Romans understood that grace extended beyond forgiveness of their past sins to forgiveness of their future sins. They understood that sin cannot master the Christian since we are not under law, but under grace (Romans 6:14). But they were drawing erroneous conclusions from this base that would lead them back to death (Romans 6:14-16).

Paul's purpose in Romans 6 is to counter this error. However, he does not disagree with their basic premise that we are free from sin, but corrects their line of reasoning and their conclusion. His methodology is to reason from their good knowledge of what happens at baptism to the correct conclusion that God intended for them thereafter to "walk in newness of life" and to consider themselves "to be dead to sin" (Romans 6:4, 11). The Romans knew they had died to sin at baptism. Once again Paul makes this clear when he corrects their erroneous conclusion by two more rhetorical questions: "How shall we who died to sin still live in it? Or do you not know that all of us who have been baptized into Christ Jesus have been baptized into His death?" (Romans 6:2, 3). Paul was not educating these Roman Christians to know that the place and the moment of their liberation from sin was at baptism; they knew that. Their understanding of that truth is inherent in the nature of the rhetorical questions. Paul's point in these questions is that we are not only freed (justified) from sin at baptism (Romans 6:7), but that we die to sin at baptism. Since dead men do not live, men who have died to sin do not live in sin. Paul further reasons on the ground of the truth that they know to the correct conclusion: that inasmuch as we are united with Christ in baptism, which is a likeness of Christ's death, the body of sin is therefore to be done away. The remarkable result of this death to sin is then declared: "that our body of sin might be done away with, so that we would no longer be slaves to sin" (Romans 6:5, 6). Yes, the condition of being free from sin is that we die to sin as a lifestyle. But the basic truth which emerges from Paul's line of reasoning is that when Christ sets sinners free from sin, He intends to keep them free from sin.

After teaching the Galatians, "It was for freedom that Christ set us free," he then warns them against a misapplication of this wonderful truth: "For you were called to freedom, brethren; only do not turn your freedom into an opportunity for the flesh" (Galatians 5:13). The basic truth in both Galatians and Romans, regarding that from which we have been set free, is freedom from sin.

B. CHRISTIANS ARE TO MAINTAIN THAT FREEDOM

1. "**Stand fast**." This is the required human element in the ongoing nature of justification by faith. We came into freedom by an obedience of faith (Galatians 3:26, 27), and we will "stand fast" in that freedom by a continual obedience of faith.

2. "**Do not be subject again to a yoke of slavery**." The term *yoke* strongly hints of the language of Peter when, at the Jerusalem conference, he spoke of the law as "a yoke which neither our fathers nor we have been able to bear" (Acts 15:10). Why could they not bear the yoke of the law of Moses? Some answer that it is impossible for man to keep the law perfectly, that it is too difficult a requirement to bear. However, the Scripture says of the law that it is "not too difficult for you" (Deuteronomy 30:11). We are responsible for our sins. It is the law's purpose to convict us of our guilt. But responsible men are nevertheless inveterate sinners (1 John 1:10). The law, then, requiring sinless perfection, became an unbearable yoke to those who appealed to it for salvation, for by its nature it can only condemn. Therefore the law yokes men to their sins and pronounces upon them the curse of death. It is from this indictment of sin-guiltiness and the curse of death that Christ delivered these Gentile

Christians (Galatians 3:13), and it is to this curse they would "again" return if they put themselves under the law of Moses. These Gentile Christians were never under the law to be subject to it "again." But if they placed themselves, by conviction, under it they would be "subject again to a yoke of slavery" (the law itself) that could not free them from their future sins anymore than their former idolatry which held them in slavery to their sin. Hence the law of Moses yokes men to the slavery of their sins. In this way, because of the law's requirement of sinless perfection and because of the law's nature to condemn the sinner, the law became an unbearable yoke of bondage to anyone who would place himself under it.

Paul's point is that the Galatians were freed from the law's curse of sin and death, and that they were not to place themselves under the law inasmuch as it would curse them for their future sins. Because the Galatians, and all men, have an inveterate proneness to sin even after justification, the law, or any other system than justification by faith in Christ, would become to them, and to us, a yoke of bondage.

Thank God for Jesus Christ who has given Christians the victory over sin and death. Sin shall have no dominion over us; for we are not under law, but under grace. We have been freed from sin for freedom from sin. Stand fast therefore and do not be subject again to a yoke of slavery to sin.

II. Consequences of Legalism, 5:2-6

Behold I, Paul, say to you that if you receive circumcision, Christ will be of no benefit to you. And I testify again to every man who receives circumcision, that he is under obligation to keep the whole Law. You have been severed from Christ, you who are seeking to be justified by law; you have fallen from grace. For we through the Spirit, by faith, are waiting for the hope of righteousness. For in Christ Jesus neither circumcision nor uncircumcision means anything, but faith working through love (Galatians 5:2-6).

With his "Behold I, Paul, say to you," Paul now speaks with the authority of his apostleship. He speaks of the consequences of legalism resulting from the false teaching at Galatia.

A. CONSEQUENCES, 5.2-4

1. **Christ will be of no benefit to you**. How can Christ be of any benefit to the Christian if He becomes of no benefit? The theology that a sinner once saved by grace cannot lose his salvation for any reason denies the undeniable. No benefit does not allow for any benefit. To say that Christ will be of no benefit to you and at the same time affirm that you do have the benefit of salvation is to reduce language to meaninglessness. Paul states that the consequence of this Galatian legalism, which is tantamount to trusting in the wrong person, is to place their sinful selves under the curse of the law. Belief in the impossibility of apostasy seems to be the consequence of an inadequate theology that does not allow for the full definition of saving faith. While obedience of faith earns nothing it is obedience that perfects our faith (James 2:20-24). Not perfect obedience, but an obedient lifestyle and a continual struggle against sin and self. Accordingly Scripture says, "Be faithful until death, and I will give you the crown of life" (Revelation 2:10).

2. **Under obligation to keep the whole law**. This is due to the nature of the law of Moses that required sinless observance and condemned the violator at the first infraction. As Paul observed, "For as many as are of the works of the Law are under a curse; for it is written, 'Cursed is everyone who does not abide by all things written in the Book of the Law, to perform them' (Galatians 3:10 quoting Deuteronomy 27:26). If the Galatians placed themselves under the law they assumed the obligation to keep it perfectly or to be condemned (cursed) immediately upon the first infraction. Since men will sin those under the law will be cursed.

   Legalism is a lie. It affirms the impossible; it offers a system that condemns sinners as if it were a system of salvation for sinners! Both legalists and their converts expose themselves in the light of God's Word as greatly lacking in the knowledge of the gospel as well as in the knowledge of the nature of law.

3. **Will be severed from Christ**. Alternative translations for "severed" are "discharged," "alienated," and "estranged." As Bruce says, "your association with Christ has been nullified. Compare the same verb used in the opposite sense in Rom. 7:6... 'we have been released from the law.' Circumcision would be 'the sacrament of their excision from Christ.'"[1]

4. **You have fallen from grace**. The gospel message is that salvation is by God's grace through our faith in Christ. If the sinner places his faith in the wrong person or thing, he cannot by that means have access to God's saving grace. Only Christ is our access to God (Ephesians 2:18), and He becomes our access only when we place our faith in Him (Romans 5:1, 2). Consequently if a Christian places his faith for justification in another, he will fall from grace, he will become estranged from Christ, alienated from Him as he was before salvation (as when Paul reminded the Ephesians of their former condition before their salvation; they were "separate" or "excluded from the commonwealth of Israel," meaning that "at that time" they had "no hope" and were "without God in the world" (Ephesians 2:11, 12). Bruce further comments on this passage: "God had called the Galatians...(1:6); to forsake his call for the way of law involved self-expulsion from his grace, because they no longer relied on it."[2] See also Romans 11:19-22; Hebrews 3:12-14; 10:26-30.

   Salvation cannot be earned; Christ did that for us. It is by grace, but it is not a cheap grace that costs us nothing. Scripture teaches it must be accepted by obedience of faith (Romans 1:5; 16:25, 26). After justification, salvation remains conditional; we must maintain our faith in Christ, we must maintain an obedient lifestyle, and not place our faith in another person or in another system.

B. REASONS FOR THE CONSEQUENCES, 5:5, 6

1. **"For."** In the original this post positive word introduces the reason to be given.

2. **Christians wait through the Spirit by faith for the hope of righteousness**
   a. "**Wait**." That is, wait patiently by steadfast Christian living for the hope of eternal life that our imputed righteousness, that is, our justification, has guaranteed to us.
   b. "**Through the Spirit by faith**." What we do through the Spirit we do by faith. Paul will tell us in this chapter to "walk by the Spirit" (5:16). But he also says that "we walk by faith" (2 Corinthians 5:7). Now the question: do we walk by the Spirit, or do we walk by faith? Paul tells us that "we live by the Spirit" (Galatians 5:25), but he also tells us that we "live by faith in the Son of God" (Galatians 2:20). How, then, do we live? By the Spirit or by faith in Christ? Paul explains, "faith comes from hearing, and hearing by the word of Christ" (Romans 10:17). To walk by faith and to live by faith is to walk and to live by the Spirit's Word. Ultimately it is only through the Spirit's written Word that we learn of Christ. It is by the Scriptures that the Spirit generates faith in Christ. It is by His Word we learn how to trust Christ and what it means to live by faith in Him. We know nothing of Christ's life, personality, nature, mission, what was accomplished in His death, or of His resurrection, or of His teachings outside of the Bible, the Spirit's written Word. Paul also says that "all who are being led by the Spirit of God, these are sons of God" (Romans 8:14). But how does the Spirit lead us if not by His Word? Providentially, yes, as in answer to prayer. But the Spirit leads sinners and Christians to faith in Christ by His Word, not by any other means. He leads us by His Word to know what we as sinners are to do to be saved. And He leads us by His Word to know what it is to "live by faith in Christ." This is what Christ affirmed (John 17:20), and the prophets and Paul (Romans 10:13-17).

   Keep in mind that when Paul said, "We through the Spirit, by faith, are waiting for the hope of righteousness," he offers this as a reason for detailing the consequences of legalism. Legalism severs us from Christ because it does not place faith in Christ as the Holy Spirit teaches. Legalism is not taught by the Spirit either in the law or in the New Testament. The Holy Spirit has always taught justification by faith. Paul affirms that the Holy Spirit will not lead anyone to come under law (5:18). Accordingly, when Paul said, "For we through the Spirit, by faith..." he was saying that the Lord teaches that our hope is based on faith in Christ, not in flesh-power under the law. So listen to the Lord in both the Old Testament and the New Testament and you will not be deceived into believing that salvation comes by law.

c. **"The hope of righteousness**." Paul seems to be speaking of the thing hoped for, eternal life, and that hope is based on our confidence that God has accounted our faith for righteousness. We have a living hope of an inheritance that cannot be defiled and will not fade away (1 Peter 1:3, 4). This hope is not based on law. It is based confidently on Christ. We are patiently and faithfully waiting for that hope which our imputed righteousness in Christ guarantees. The Christian's hope, based on the confidence that he is justified, is a dynamic motivation to live for God while we live in tension with the world.

3. **In Christ, neither circumcision nor uncircumcision means anything**. Paul has already said that we are all one man in Christ regardless of race or gender (Galatians 3:28). Circumcision counts for absolutely nothing now that Christ has come. Nor does uncircumcision count against a man at all. Neither circumcision, nor ethnic background, nor financial nor social standing, nor education nor lack of it, nor who we know or who knows us, nor what we have accomplished or how we have suffered - none of this counts for justification. But faith in Christ working by love, that counts for everything and is reckoned for righteousness.

III. Legalism's Fallacies, 5:7-12

You were running well; who hindered you from obeying the truth? This persuasion did not come from Him who calls you. A little leaven leavens the whole lump of dough. I have confidence in you in the Lord that you will adopt no other view; but the one who is disturbing you will bear his judgment, whoever he is. But I, brethren, if I still preach circumcision, why am I still persecuted? Then the stumbling block of the cross has been abolished. I wish that those who are troubling you would even mutilate themselves (Galatians 5:7-12).

A. LEGALISM HINDERS OBEDIENCE, 5:7

This part of the letter makes the disturbance mentioned at the beginning of the letter (1:7) a bit clearer. Paul indicates that if the Galatians were left alone they would throw off Judaism and continue in their obedience to the truth (5:10). After all, they "were running well," to use an appropriate athletic term. But the Judaizers continued to agitate the churches until they became uncertain of their course and ceased to obey the truth. Paul may have used another athletic term when he asked rhetorically, "Who cut in on you?" as if to ask, "Who hindered you from continuing to run the race?" (cf. 1 Corinthians 9:24-27). Had some of the Galatians become disheartened, discouraged? Under the requirement of the law had they begun to feel that their religion was too hard? Legalism had become an obstacle to these brethren; they had ceased to be obedient.

Legalism bears its predictable, natural fruit by paralyzing us through uncertainty. This is one of the two manifestations of legalism. It either produces an arrogant, judgmental self-confidence (as in Luke 18:9-14) or a paralyzing uncertainty born of insecurity.

B. LEGALISM IS NOT FROM GOD, 5:8

A principle to remember is that if a doctrine hinders obedience of faith to Christ, it is not of God and is to be jettisoned when recognized. "Cast out the bondwoman and her son."

C. LEGALISM CORRUPTS THE ENTIRE BODY OF CHRIST, 5:9

Like leaven in dough, it grows. It will not go away if left alone. Sometimes we have to purge out the old leaven (1 Corinthians 5:6-8) to keep the body sound, unified, and productive. Sometimes we have to defend the truth of the gospel, as in the Galatian letter.

D. LEGALISM COMPROMISES THE GOSPEL, 5:11

It removes the need for the cross (as in Galatians 2:21). The cross was itself a scandal (*skandalon*), as only the worst of criminals were crucified. The Jews, even the disciples closest to Christ, due to their nationalistic concept of the prophesied kingdom (cf. Matthew 11:12; John 6:15; Mark 10:35-38), were unable to understand the plain unveiled language of the Lord that He was to be crucified (Luke 9:44, 45; 18:31-34). Their theological presuppositions would not allow them to harmonize the cross of Christ into their religion (cf. 1 Corinthians 1:18-25). The legalistic concept of justification by flesh-power compromised the gospel message by divesting it of the need for the cross. The legalist may offer lip-service to the cross, but it is not the ground of his confidence for salvation. Legalism simply does not understand the cross by grace and justification by faith.

When today we pervert Christian obedience into merit and fail to see the cross as the ground of our acceptance before God we compromise the gospel and pervert the good news into a message of mere legalism. The upshot will be a mixture of uncertainty, insecurity, and paralysis amid arrogance, hypercriticism, and judgmentalism (as in James 2:4).

E. LEGALISM MUTILATES THE GOSPEL, 5:12

As just observed, legalism cuts the cross out of the gospel. That, of course, is perversion (Galatians 1:6, 7), cutting the good news right out of the message. Paul's disgust with this legalism, and the Holy Spirit's who guided him, led him to use a grim illustration of the logical conclusion that such a doctrine naturally embraces. The Galatians were located near Phrygia, which was the center of the worship of Cybele, the Great Mother of the gods. That worship involved fertility rites during which the priests, in a frenzy, made themselves eunuchs. What the Judaizers were teaching essentially agreed with those pagan priests, differing from their practice only in degree. Paul seems to say that for the Judaizers to be consistent they should actually castrate themselves. He even seems to wish that they would in hopes that such practice would startle the Galatians into the realization of the perversion of such legalism.

CONCLUSION: The freedom Christians have from the guilt of sin is by faith in the person and work of Christ Jesus. When that faith leads a sinner to renounce his life of sin and takes Jesus to be the Lord of his life and to be baptized into Christ, that person is justified, he is freed from sin (Romans 6:1-7). And the Lord has freed him to remain free from the guilt of sin. But the ongoing nature of justification is conditional. It is conditioned on keeping faith in Christ. Paul pleads with the Galatians, and us, not to return to the bondage of our sins again by yoking ourselves to any other person or system that takes faith out of Christ. The consequences are fatal. So even as we were set free from sin by an obedience of faith in Christ, we are to stand fast in our freedom from sin by a continual obedience of faith in Christ. Stand fast therefore.

Spiritual Probing
Chapter Eleven

1. The final two chapters of Galatians are called The Practical Section. How does the fact that the first four chapters are written in the indicative mood and the last two chapters are written in the imperative mood highlight the practicality of these closing chapters?

2. Were the Galatian Gentile Christians ever under the law of Moses prior to the coming of the Judaizers? Paul says they were freed for freedom. From what, then, were they set free (Galatians 5:1)? For what freedom were they set free? To what bondage would they have returned if they had espoused the law? How would the law have yoked them to that bondage? Can Christians today return through legalism to their old bondage of sin? Illustrate that.

3. Galatians teaches by principle that mere human inventions, like the rituals of Pagan, Islamic, Hindu, and Catholic religions, are too "weak and worthless" to make a sinner right with God. Such ritual practice is legalism. Can we pervert the works of faith, like soul winning, the Lord's supper, and worship attendance into mere ritual legalism and trust ourselves to keep enough commandments to be acceptable to God? According to Galatians 4:9 and 5:2-4 what would be the outcome of such practice?

4. Paul explains that if Christians put faith in law keeping, or, by principle, in mere ritual (whether human or Christian), they sever themselves from Christ and fall from saving grace. Can you explain why? Galatians 2:16 and 3:26 tell why.

5. Paul said that the law of Moses was holy, righteous, and good (Romans 7:12). Why, then, did Peter say, at the Jerusalem conference, that the law was an unbearable yoke? See Acts 15:10.

6. Can men who are not under the law of Moses be cursed by that law? Romans 3:19-20 can help. What is that curse?

7. Was it an impossible human task to keep the law of Moses? What does Deuteronomy 30:11-14 say about that? Since no man other than Christ has ever kept the law, what does that say about man?

8. Is the faithful, trusting Christian free from the condemnation of his future sins? See Galatians 5:1; Romans 6:3-7; 8:1-3; 1 John 1:7, 9; 2:1, 2.

9. Can an unfaithful Christian be alienated from Christ, be severed from Christ, and fall from saving grace? See Galatians 5:2-4. How, then, can Christians be free from their future sins?

10. What does Paul mean: We through the Spirit, by faith, are waiting for the hope of righteousness?

11. How does legalism compromise the gospel? Can you identify such compromises today?

The Liberated Lifestyle of the Spirit-Guided Man
Galatians 5:13-26

Christian freedom is not merely theoretical, it is intensely practical. To bring practicality to his message the apostle raises upon the foundation of his gospel theology the superstructure of a corresponding Christian lifestyle. Paul now seeks to commit the Galatian churches to a life that is commensurate with a mature faith in Christ. Charles Cousar tells us that in Galatians 5:13-6:10 there are no less than fifteen imperatives or implied imperatives in the Greek text by which Paul urges his precious children to exercise their new-found freedom responsibly.[1]

I. Christian Freedom Must Not Be Perverted Into License, 5:13-15

For you were called to freedom, brethren; only do not turn your freedom into an opportunity for the flesh, but through love serve one another. For the whole Law is fulfilled in one word, in the statement, "You shall love your neighbor as yourself." But if you bite and devour one another, take care that you are not consumed by one another (Galatians 5:13-15).

Paul knows that men are often characterized by extremes. How much more these unstable Galatians. If up to this point in his epistle, thinks Paul, the Galatians have been persuaded that legalism is in fact a fatal error, there yet seems to remain a potential swing to license that must also be addressed.

A. FREEDOM'S RESPONSIBILITY

Freedom from sin is not a license to indulge the desires of the flesh. True, we have been delivered from the law of sin and death;

as we sin He condemns our sin (Romans 8:1-3). But we must not forget that this is conditioned on our willingness from the heart to walk after the Spirit's directives (Romans 8:4; 1 John 1:7). This will not be the only time Paul anticipates an excessive misapplication of the Christian's freedom (Romans 6:1, 2). Apparently there will ever be the subjective reasoning that if we are free from sin then we can sin with freedom from punishment. God forbid!

Galatians does not emphasize, as do libertines, what we are free to do. But it is strong on what we are free from. We are free from the condemnation of law, from the guilt and penalty of sin, and from separation from God. But we are not free to do as we please. As Christ's freemen we are at the same time bondslaves to Him to walk in righteousness (Romans 6:15-18; I Peter 2:16, 17). As a condition for entering into the kingdom, the new reign of God through Christ, we had to experience a new birth (John 3:3-8) that is fully intended to issue in a new lifestyle in imitation of Christ. A condition of our justification and continued freedom is an obedience of faith that repents from sin and repents toward God (Acts 2:38; 20:21). Repentance, the change of mind, heart, and will, will result in a life-change that is directed by the Word of God and empowered by His indwelling Holy Spirit.

B. LOVE IS THE ALTERNATIVE TO LAW

The need for the liberation of a totally enslaved humanity and the gospel of God's inexpressible love seems too often to be interpreted in our sin-dulled perceptions as excessive overstatements. Satan, through a post-modern conception of Christianity that mitigates absolutes into uncertainties, would have us think that the gap between what we are and what we ought to be is not all that wide. Paul's exhortation in this section of the epistle to a radical change of Christian concept leading to a radical change of lifestyle exhibits the wideness of the gap that actually exists between the world's conception of right and wrong and the reality of that conception. In another epistle he stresses that "the grace of God...instructing us to deny ungodliness and worldly desires and to live sensibly, righteously and godly in this present age" (Titus 2:11-12). In yet another epistle he standardizes that lifestyle as an oughtness of the required Christian behavior (1 Timothy 3:14-15). The idea that we may need a little changing here and there, but not a total renewal of concept and lifestyle is at odds with Christ's own teaching of a new birth as requisite to both enabling us to perceive the nature of the kingdom of God and for actually entering into it (John 3:3-5). Consequently, a realistic view of the extremity of sin's perversion of human nature and conscience and of man's desperate need for regeneration are from this false perspective greatly diminished. Sinful men are experts in the art of self-defense against the charge, even from God, that they are terribly contaminated and degenerated by sin. Although God will accept a faith-response from such sinners, the initial motivation in such cases seems to be more of self-preservation than of reciprocal love. This selfishness, this worldly baggage, when carried over from the old life into the church, is often productive of the immature infighting that consumes one another (5:13-15). History and human experience combine to justify Paul's anticipation of our need to love one another. His statement that "the whole Law is fulfilled in one word, 'You shall love your neighbor as yourself,'" is not mere obedience to some specific law, but a total approach to life.

Our new lifestyle is not only in relation to God, but is essentially a "one another" relationship. Paul has just connected love to faith (5:6). Now he connects love to our freedom. We love God, who loves us, by loving those whom He loves (1 John 4:7-11, 20). We just do not love God if we do not love our brethren. Consequently, Paul writes, "do not turn your freedom into an opportunity for the flesh, but through love serve one another." Most people have an experiential knowledge that law is not productive of obedience from the heart. Our school zones are marked by reduced speed limits to protect our children from injury. We observe the automobiles and the cycles slowing just outside the speed zones, only to lurch forward again just outside the zone at the other end. We know that is mere obedience to the letter of the law. But parents need no such laws to protect their precious children. They are motivated by love to drive their vehicles ever so carefully.

There is, then, the working principle that love accomplishes what law cannot. When Christian love finally reciprocates out of an ever-increasing gratitude for our incredible Liberator and for our liberation from the extreme depths of our contamination, it will interpret our freedom to place ourselves in genuine servitude to each other. This will be no more than an imitation of Christ whose eternal love led the way.

C. FREEDOM'S REALITY

If Paul's words are received as the very words of God, and if Christians take his word at face value, will that not produce the ecstasy that comes to slaves at their liberation, and sadly is sometimes translated into a careless attitude towards others? For that reason Paul seeks to responsibly direct that freedom lest it be perverted to the destruction of our own brethren. But he does not intend to diminish freedom's reality. Paul has not overstated the case. Sin actually has no dominion over us, for we are not under the condemnation of a legal system. Those walking by faith in Christ are actually free from the law of sin and death. Our faith has indeed been reckoned for righteousness. Our sins are not reckoned against us. God actually condemns our sins as we walk in the light of the Spirit's Word. Paul intends his words to be taken at face value: "It was for freedom that Christ set us free...For you were called to freedom, brethren." The reality is that Christians have been freed for freedom. When faith led to baptism we were freed from the guilt and penalty of all our past sins to be kept free from the guilt and penalty of all future sins. Freed for freedom! This gospel reality is a dynamic that will eventually mature into a selfless lifestyle that is more an expression of gratitude to a wonderful loving Savior than of mere grudging obedience to law.

II. What It Is To Walk By the Spirit, 5:16-18

But I say, walk by the Spirit, and you will not carry out the desire of the flesh. For the flesh sets its desire against the Spirit, and the Spirit against the flesh; for these are in opposition to one another, so that you may not do the things that you please. But if you are led by the Spirit, you are not under the Law (Galatians 5:16-18).

This part of the letter is well-known for a presentation of the contrast between the kind of lifestyle the flesh wants to live and the lifestyle into which the Spirit of Christ would guide us. Paul's "But I say, walk by the Spirit, and you will not carry out the desire of the flesh" naturally comes out of the foregoing. The lifestyle of Christ's freeman is directed by the Spirit into love of the brethren. The desire of the flesh is subordinated to the Spirit. What is it, then, to walk by the Spirit?

A. WALKING BY THE SPIRIT IS NOT SUBJECTIVISM

God's love for us steers us away from a course directed by our feelings, as though these are the Spirit's urgings. God, knowing the propensity of man to follow after his own heart into error, has warned us to be directed by His Word (Numbers 15:37-40). He has warned us that a way that seems right could nevertheless be the course of death (Proverbs 14:12) and that we cannot determine God's intended course for man by some existential experience (Jeremiah 10:23).

B. IT IS FOLLOWING AFTER THE SPIRIT'S TEACHING

However God may guide us through our Christian lives in answer to prayer, by agents other than God's Word, whether by the ministration of angels (Hebrews 1:14) or by human instrumentalities, such guidance is providentially brought about. But acts of God's providence are to be distinguished from acts of divine revelation. By the special work of revelation upon the apostles and New Testament prophets the Holy Spirit made known the gospel and God's will for men (Ephesians 3:3-5). Then by the special means of inspiration, He had the revealed Word written into permanent record. This Word claims to be sufficient (2 Corinthians 3:5, 6; 2 Timothy 3:16, 17) and final (Jude 3) as the means of our instruction. What other means has God furnished us than His Spirit-revealed Word by which we can objectively know the way in which the Spirit would direct us to walk? The idea that we are to yield to both the Spirit's promptings opens the door to equating the fallible interpretations of our subjective feelings with the Spirit's guidance. Again we must echo the wisdom of God, "There is a way which seems right to a man, but its end is the way of death" (Proverbs 14:12). It is by the means of His Word that He saves us, bears His fruit in our lives, and directs us into our Christian walk.

1. **The Spirit saves us by the Word of the gospel**. Both Christ and Paul tell us that the Holy Spirit has a part in our new birth, in our renewal (John 3:5; Titus 3:5). At the same time Paul says the Corinthian Christians were begotten by the gospel (1 Corinthians 4:15). Is it, then, by the Spirit or by the gospel that God saves us? It is, of course, by the Spirit's gospel. James, employing the analogy of birth, tells us that according to God's own will, we are "brought...forth" by His Word (James 1:18). The apostle Peter writes that "you have been born again not of seed which is perishable but imperishable, that is, through the living and enduring word of God" (1 Peter 1:23). Obviously the Spirit saves us, regenerates us, begats us again, by the Word of the gospel. We are also saved by faith in Christ. But since faith comes by hearing the Word of Christ (Romans 10:17) it is conclusive that the Spirit saves sinners by the Word of the gospel as it produces an obedience of faith in Christ. The Spirit both directs us into Christ by His Word and directs us to walk in Christ by His Word.

2. **The Spirit bears His fruit by His Word**. Paul tells us that "the fruit of the Spirit is love, joy, peace, patience, kindness, goodness, faithfulness, gentleness, self-control" (5:22, 23). How does the Spirit produce this fruit? We know that the Spirit teaches us in other New Testament passages to observe each of these named fruits as characteristics of Christ, to be gentle, to be patient, to love one another (Ephesians 4:1, 2), to exercise self-control (2 Peter 1:6), to be faithful (Revelation 2:10), etc. Does the Holy Spirit add something of His own to the production of this fruit when we obey Him? While the Bible does not explicitly say so, it implies as much. We know from Scripture that God gives us growth and development when we cooperate with Him (cf. Ephesians 4:11-16). Is this growth providentially accomplished by

the Spirit working within? Ephesians 3:16 leads us to believe it. But the Spirit initiates that fruit-bearing by His teaching.

3. **The Spirit guides us by His Word**. We must make a distinction between what the Spirit does and what we do. The Spirit personally indwells God's people (Galatians 4:6; Romans 8:9). He intercedes for us when we pray (Romans 8:26), strengthens us in the inner man (Ephesians 3:16), and will one day raise His own from the dead (Romans 8:11). This is what the Spirit does. But walking by the Spirit is what *we* do. Apart from the revelation of the Spirit's Word, we know nothing of the gospel or of God's will for us in Christ. To walk by the Spirit is tantamount to walking in the light of His Word (as in 1 John 1:7). Paul has already said that what we do by the Spirit we do by faith (Galatians 5:5). Since faith comes by hearing the Word, what we do by the Spirit through faith we do by His Word. When Paul tells us to "walk by the Spirit" he tells us to walk according to His teaching.

Christians today must be careful not to equate Scriptures that speak of the indwelling of the Spirit with the Spirit's guidance. The indwelling Spirit guides us to be sure, but we know that He indwells us and what His directives are only by His Word. God tells us that there is more than our own obedience working in our behalf (e.g., the intercession of the Spirit during prayer and His strengthening of our inner man), but, we have no authority to substitute the objective Word of God with some spiritual existentialism as a revelation from the Spirit.

C. WALKING BY THE SPIRIT IS NOT TO BE LED UNDER A LEGAL LAW.

No Scripture speaks of man's inability to keep the law. Man may deduct that conclusion; he may marshal Scriptures for a theology by which he claims to "prove it." But no Scripture states it. To the contrary, Moses writes after a restatement of the law to Israel, "For this commandment which I command you today is not too difficult for you, nor is it out of reach....But the word is very near you, in your mouth and in your heart, that you may observe it" (Deuteronomy 30:11-14).

Scripture does teach, however, that man is unable to come into a right relationship with God through the law because of man's sin and the law's nature to condemn the sinner. The Holy Spirit, then, will not lead the Christian under the law to his condemnation (Galatians 5:18). The law is an unbearable yoke to sinful men who would appeal to it for justification precisely because of man's sin and the law's nature to condemn it, but not because man is unable to keep it. God is not responsible for man's sins by giving him a law unable to be observed. Man is morally responsible for his sins. He is guilty before God. But while one sin brings condemnation, God's love provides redemption from sin conditioned on our faith in Christ and our willingness to wage a sincere struggle against the flesh. While walking by the Spirit is not sinless perfection, God nevertheless accounts the faithful Christian walk as a perfect fulfillment of the law's requirement (Romans 8:4). This is the astonishing message of the gospel of salvation by faith in Christ.

III. Walking By the Spirit Versus Walking By the Flesh, 5:19-26

The Spirit of Christ will not lead us to a legal system (5:18), for that would be our undoing through our sinful flesh. Nor will the Spirit lead us to indulge the desires of the flesh (5:17). He will lead us through His Word into a participation of His own divine nature, the nature of Christ. The difference between these natures is distinctive, like an open book for all to read.

A. THE FLESH-GUIDED MAN

Now the deeds of the flesh are evident, which are: immorality, impurity, sensuality, idolatry, sorcery, enmities, strife, jealousy, outbursts of anger, disputes, dissensions, factions, envying, drunkenness, carousing, and things like these, of which I forewarn you, just as I have forewarned you, that those who practice such things will not inherit the kingdom of God (Galatians 5:19-21).

1. **The flesh.** In this instance the flesh is man's sinful nature. The fleshly, carnal, or "natural man" (1 Corinthians 2:14) is

governed by his fleshly desires. Such a person "does not accept the things of the Spirit of God" (the gospel things revealed by the Spirit to the apostles and conveyed to us through their word, 1 Corinthians 2:10-14).

2. **The works of the flesh**. This way of life is as evident as the wreckage and ruin it produces. These works of the flesh can be placed into four categories:

   a. Sexual: immorality, impurity, sensuality
   b. Religious: idolatry, sorcery (witchcraft)
   c. Social or inter-relational: enmities, strife, jealousy, carousing
   d. Substance abuse: drunkenness

3. "**Things like these**." When Paul speaks of "things like these," he clearly indicates that he has not exhausted the list of fleshly deeds. By naming fifteen distinctive deeds of the flesh and then warning us that those who practice "such things" shall not inherit the kingdom of God, he asks us to make our own list. Clearly, God expects us to have enough intellectual and spiritual insight from the outset to identify and crucify (5:24) "such things" of the flesh. The Spirit-led man will by practice along these guidelines train his senses "to discern good and evil" (Hebrews 5:14).

4. **Practice such things**. Paul writes that those who practice such things shall not inherit the kingdom of God. There is a difference between a practice and an act, between a settled course of action and an isolated incident. John indicates that even as Christians we will sin (1 John 1:10), and some of those sins will be committed even while we are making dedicated efforts to walk in the light (1 John 1:7). But Christians who are walking by the Spirit are not practicing the "deeds of the flesh." We sin, but we also struggle against sin. We are crucifying the flesh. We both desire to and try to observe all things whatsoever Christ has commanded. The Spirit and the flesh are in opposition to one another, and he who walks by the Spirit is not doing the things that please the flesh (5:17). Though imperfect he is not practicing "such things" of the flesh.

John writes that for Christians not every sin leads to death (1 John 5:16, 17). There is sin that leads even Christians to death, but not every sin. This is not to be interpreted as though there are certain sins that are allowed and the rest are not. The difference here is between the attitude of one who is willing to struggle against the flesh to do righteousness, out of faith in Christ, and one who resigns himself to the practice of what he knows to be sin. Not every sin is a sin unto death because Christ paid the price of our sins at the cross and thereby provided a rescue from our sinfulness by justification. God is satisfied with Christ's sin-offering for every sin we have ever committed or will commit. But this redemption is on the condition that we renounce sin as a way of life, place our trust in Jesus as sin-offering, and espouse the Spirit-led life as over against the life of the flesh.

5. **"Will not inherit the kingdom of God**." The "kingdom of God" usually refers to the reign of God over the lives of His people, to which reign His church is of a trusting disposition to submit. But here the "kingdom" appears to embrace more than God's sovereign dominion, for Paul speaks of the kingdom as the object of our inheritance. This is reminiscent of Peter's instruction to practice the deeds that characterize the divine nature (2 Peter 1:5-11), by which means "entrance into the eternal kingdom of our Lord and Savior Jesus Christ will be abundantly supplied to you." Though Christians are presently residents in the kingdom of God (Colossians 1:12, 13; Revelation 1:6; 5:9, 10) there is a God to glorify, a mission to be accomplished, a battle to be waged to the death. Then shall be supplied to us entrance into that phase of the kingdom after which all such wrestlings cease.

B. THE SPIRIT-GUIDED MAN

But the fruit of the Spirit is love, joy, peace, patience, kindness, goodness, faithfulness, gentleness, self-control; against such things there is no law. Now those who belong to Christ Jesus have crucified the flesh with its passions and desires. If we live by the Spirit, let us also walk by the Spirit. Let us not become boastful, challenging one another, envying one another (Galatians 5:22-26).

While the deeds of the flesh are usually quite evident the fruit of the Spirit takes time to flower and grow into full bloom. The word *fruit* carries the idea of growth. Paul speaks in another place of Christians under the tutelage of spiritual leaders in the local churches who "are no longer to be children, tossed here and there by waves and carried about by every wind of doctrine, by the trickery of men, by craftiness in deceitful scheming; but speaking the truth in love, we are to grow up in all aspects into Him, who is the head, even Christ" (Ephesians 4:11-15).

A man may espouse Christ in all sincerity and bend his will to follow after the Spirit. At the same time it is so often the case that he does not perceive in himself the satanic contamination of his former life that is carried over into the new life - his dogmatism, his legalism, his arrogance and pride, his insensitivity to the feelings of others. Paul and Peter address these very practices in their letters to those who are partaking of grace. To crucify "the flesh with its passions and desires" and to bear the fruit of the Spirit requires an objective look at oneself in the mirror of the Spirit's Word (James 1:23-25) and a constant struggle to walk by the Spirit as opposed to the flesh. But the result is certain - first the bud, then the flower, then at last the fruit.

Paul encourages us that against the fruit of the Spirit "there is no law." Our freedom in Christ releases us, not only from sin and its condemnation, but from the gnawing uncertainty of our eternal destiny. Faithful, Spirit-led Christians are confident of their salvation, and are therefore free from the anxiety that paralyzes those who would walk by the Spirit, but through insecurity have no motivating strength to carry through. Christ's confident freeman can practice his walk with the Spirit ever so imperfectly without giving up. In spite of his imperfections he is motivated to keep on keeping on.

CONCLUSION: The message of the gospel is that if we by faith in Christ practice walking by the Spirit, we can have the confidence of our salvation that will motivate us to a greater life of holiness and to higher attainments of spiritual insight and development. "If we live by the Spirit, let us also walk by the Spirit."

Spiritual Probing
Chapter Twelve

1. Men are characterized by extremes. What extreme does Paul address in Galatians 5:13-26 now that legalism has been addressed?
2. Illustrate how genuine Christian love can accomplish what law cannot. Can this be applied to the love we have for our wonderful Savior to the extent that we will actually want to be obedient as an expression of our deep gratitude?
3. How does the Christian know when he is walking by the Spirit? Is this a subjective or an objective matter?
4. Paul says that if a man is under law he cannot be under the leading of the Spirit (Galatians 5:18). Explain why this is so.
5. Paul says that we are not to practice "such things" of the flesh as he names in Galatians 5:19-21. Name "such things" in today's world that are not specified in Scripture but that are necessarily implied. Perhaps it would help to identify them in their separate categories: sexual, religious, social or inter-relational, and substance abuse.
6. Galatians teaches that believers have been freed for freedom. At the same time it teaches that if we practice such sins as named in Galatians 5:19-21 we will not inherit the kingdom of God. Make a distinction between a practice and an act and address this subject.
7. What does it mean that there is no law against the fruit of the Spirit (Galatians 5:22, 23)?
8. What does Paul mean to live by the Spirit (Galatians 5:25)?
9. Explain how those who belong to Christ have crucified the flesh with its passions and desires, yet they sin (5:24). Hebrews 5:11-14; John 2:1, 2; 3:4-6 apply here.
10. Why can Christians who are imperfect nevertheless have confidence that they are right with God? Can this be abused? How? Can this be falsely taught? How? Will Galatians 5:13 and Romans 6:1, 15 help?

Chapter Thirteen
Christ's Cross:
The True Motive For Serving
Galatians 6:1-18

In this final section Paul reasons for a radically new family lifestyle in Christ where members of the divine family help one another over their hardships. He teaches that the motive for this kind of fellowship is rooted not in proud flesh, but in the cross of Christ. Paul's closing statement in the preceding chapter, "Let us not become boastful, challenging one another, envying one another," is a natural lead-in to this instruction.

I. A Contrast of Spiritual and Fleshly Principles of Family Problem Solving, 6:1-5

Brethren, even if anyone is caught in any trespass, you who are spiritual, restore such a one in a spirit of gentleness; each one looking to yourself, so that you too will not be tempted. Bear one another's burdens, and thereby fulfill the law of Christ. For if anyone thinks he is something when he is nothing, he deceives himself. But each one must examine his own work, and then he will have reason for boasting in regard to himself alone, and not in regard to another. For each one will bear his own load (Galatians 6:1-5).

God's spiritual men, cross-motivated and Spirit-led, employ principles of problem solving that are very different from those who are motivated by the flesh.

A. SPIRITUAL PRINCIPLES OF FAMILY PROBLEM SOLVING

    1. **You who are spiritual**. Spiritual men are those that are led by the Spirit of Christ (Romans 8:13b-14). This leading of the Spirit is not accomplished by a subjective interpretation of religious

feelings. The Christian faith, the thing believed and the life to be led, was objectively revealed to the Galatians in words with distinctive meanings when Paul originally "preached" to them the truth of the gospel, which they understood and accordingly received by faith at baptism (1:8-9; 3:26-27). They received it with the understanding that from henceforth they were to obey "the truth" of the Christian lifestyle (5:7). Earlier Paul said, "For we through the Spirit, by faith, are waiting for the hope of righteousness" (5:5). Thus Christians, both then and now, "are waiting for the hope of righteousness" by "obeying the truth" of the Spirit's Word delivered by the apostles. Hence John's "walk in the Light" (1 John 1:7) and Paul's "walk by the Spirit" (5:16) convey the same meaning and so define the "you who are spiritual" as those being led by the light of the Spirit's Word. Consequently a wounded brother should be attended only by a family member who has matured to the spiritual level of gentleness and gospel understanding.

2. **Restore such a one**. Paul uses a hypothetical case to illustrate real and abiding family problems. A brother is "caught," or overtaken, in a trespass. The "trespass" says that he knew it was wrong when he engaged in the sinful act, but being "caught" in the trespass tells us it was not premeditated. How shall we deal with "such a one"? Shall we expose him publically with the intent of shaming him into repentance? Such a problem-solving method, though often employed by parents, business managers, school teachers, and church leaders does little more than humiliate the poor soul. Such a negative means diminishes the human spirit and may indeed inflame the brother into another negative act of defensive anger. This in turn infuriates the accuser for such a transparent attempt to justify an obvious sin. And so the satanic cycle downward is unfortunately often begun.

The word *restore* was used for setting a bone so it could heal properly and be restored to its former healthy condition. Spiritual men do not shoot their own wounded family members. The Spirit-led brother remembers the cross and his own reconciliation to God, and in the empathetic gentleness of Christ he seeks to restore the brother to Christ, not only for forgiveness, but for healing and for future spiritual health.

The spiritual principles of understanding, growing out of one's own Christian experience and gentle instruction, will accomplish what harsh condemnation cannot.

3. **Fulfill the law of Christ**. Christlike men do not require a list of rules to be crossed off as duty observes them. Such a spirit seems to miss Paul's exhortation here to imbibe the spirit of Christ's selfless life who bore the burden of our sin upon the cross. Peter echos this line of reasoning when he taught us that the very life of Christ is the Christian's law to imitate (1 Peter 2:21). In bearing one another's burdens we imitate the life of Christ and in this manner fulfill Christ's new command to love one another even as He loved us (John 13:34, 35). This seems to be "the law of Christ" that Paul here has in mind for us to fulfill.

B. THE LEGALIST'S MODUS OPERANDI

The following presentation of the fleshly man's principles of operation within the body of Christ stands in marked contrast to those of the spiritual brother.

1. **He thinks he is something else**. The fleshly man's problem-solving principles include intimidation, manipulation, and sometimes violence. He does not bear burdens; he makes them by tying up heavy burdens and laying them on men's shoulders (figuratively speaking), but as for himself he is unwilling to move them with so much as his finger (cf. Matthew 23:4). His motive, says the Lord, is self-interest: "They do all their deeds to be noticed by men" (Matthew 23:5-7). As Paul says, though they are nothing they think themselves to be something (Galatians 6:3). Rather than seeking to help the brother who is "caught in any trespass" the legalist will use the brother's sin to set himself high in the estimation of the church. He is characterized by giving wide publicity to the brother's sin. The psychology here is transparent. Such a disclosure is intended to reflect the righteousness of the one who "blew the whistle."

This kind of modus operandi, so characteristic of the church's extreme right wing, is in fact a betrayal of Christ as well as the brother whom Christ has assigned us to restore. In fact this same characteristic is very often displayed by the extreme left wing of the church, who, while decrying legalism stand knee deep in their own haughty intellectual elitism, pugnaciously accusing the right wing of belligerence and theological illiteracy.

Consider the mentality of some within covenant relationship who "caught" a woman in adultery, "in the very act" (John 8:2-11). But if she was "caught...in the very act," where is the man? They were obviously operating on a double standard. They cared not for their poor sister in Abraham, but used her sin to exalt themselves over Christ.

The spiritual brother is so attuned to the cross, because of his realization of the depth of his own sin and the distance God had to travel to save him, that he neither wants to nor does he ride high on the sins of another.

2. **In fact he is nothing.** Like the rest of us, the fault-finder is as guilty of sin as the brother he is exposing. But by the grace of our Lord Jesus Christ we would all stand condemned before God. Because I have not committed adultery does not justify my telling a lie. We are responsibly taught to expose a brother who is adamantly pursuing a course of sin that leads to death, even here hoping that the discipline will bring him back (Luke 17:3; 1 Corinthians 5:5; 2 Thessalonians 3:14). But we must make a distinction between these brethren and those "caught in a trespass" who will probably respond to gentle and sympathetic efforts at restoration. Perhaps, for the sake of the legalist who is "caught" in the trespass of hyper-criticism, or of judging with evil motives, we should, with a view toward restoring him, gently remind him that in God's sight "no man living is righteous" (Psalm 143:2), and for that very reason, rather than send us to the inferno He sent Christ to the cross.

II. Spiritual Brethren Share the Good Things of God's Providence, 6:6-10

The one who is taught the word is to share all good things with the one who teaches him. Do not be deceived, God is not mocked; for whatever a man sows, this he will also reap. For the one who sows to his own flesh will from the flesh reap corruption, but the one who sows to the Spirit will from the Spirit reap eternal life. Let us not lose heart in doing good, for in due time we will reap if we do not grow weary. So then, while we have opportunity, let us do good to all people, and especially to those who are of the household of faith (Galatians 6:6-10).

From the word *koinonia* comes our word *share*. It means to participate, to have fellowship with another by receiving or giving. The unity of this paragraph seems to center around a partnership between the teacher and those he teaches. Paul is instructing the Galatians, as he will other brethren in future letters, to support those who give themselves full time to the ministry of the gospel (Romans 15:25-27; 1 Corinthians 9:4-16; 1 Timothy 5:17, 18). First he appeals to the harvest principle of reaping what we sow. Then he cautions them not to sow to the flesh nor to grow weary of sowing. Then he applies the principle to assisting all men as we have opportunity and they have need, and especially to the members of the divine household, the church.

III. A Contrast of the Real Motives Behind the Ministries of Paul and the Lawbinders, 6:11-17

See with what large letters I am writing to you with my own hand. Those who desire to make a good showing in the flesh try to compel you to be circumcised, simply so that they will not be persecuted for the cross of Christ. For those who are circumcised do not even keep the Law themselves, but they desire to have you circumcised so that they may boast in your flesh. But may it never be that I would boast, except in the cross of our Lord Jesus Christ, through which the world has been crucified to me, and I to the world. For neither is circumcision anything, nor uncircumcision, but a new creation. And those who will walk by this rule, peace and mercy be upon them, and upon the Israel of God. From now on let no one cause trouble for me, for I bear on my body the brand-marks of Jesus (Galatians 6:11-17).

A. PAUL'S TRUE MINISTRY-MOTIVES REVEALED IN HIS LETTER, 6:11

We have already given reasons for believing Paul wrote the entire Galatian letter for he says, "See with what large letters I am writing to you with my own hand." The translation "I have written to you" is an accurate rendering of the original and is the basic reason for believing that Paul wrote the entire letter to this point. Poor eyesight as indicated in Galatians 4:15, no secretary, and the urgency of the Galatian problem would be reason enough for him to strain what eyesight he had to write to his little children in trouble in spite of his handicap.

But what is the purpose of the statement, "See with what large letters I am writing to you"? He asks them to take special note of the oversized letters. But why call attention to the obvious? Would they not see the large letters without drawing attention to them? The statement itself stands alone in this place having no apparent connection with either the foregoing or the following statements. Without a purpose it is meaningless words. There is, however, a message coming out of the facts due to this statement, and Paul wants them to "see" it. Paul was criticized by the Judaizers of not really caring for the Galatians (4:12-20). He wants them to "see" two things. First, they should "see" what genuine motives of parental feeling and care are inherent in the very writing of the letter itself. Having been written under such emotional circumstances that required the tapping of the deepest reservoirs of his perplexed and aching heart, and coupled with the challenge to write a letter by a man half blind, he took pen in hand. And in order for him to see his own literary work, he began to write with painful strokes in oversized Greek characters. Second, he wants the Galatians to consider the content of the letter. Not only the doctrinal truths, but the heart of a truly caring parent, like a mother in labor (4:19) is laid bare, his anger with their lapse into foolishness (3:1), his deep yearning to be considered their friend again and not their enemy (4:16), his perplexity because he could not be present with them so that they could hear the very tone of voice that conveyed the depth of his care (4:20). In the letter his real feelings, and therefore his real self, are touchingly revealed and are now out on the table, a public record for all to "see."

Paul was being as up front as he knew how to be. He wants them to "see" that there are no hidden motives that contradict his gospel or the content of his letter. He wants them to "see" that there is no hidden agenda to bind on them later.

B. TRUE MOTIVES OF THE LEGALISTS, 6:12, 13

1. **Personal glory motives**. Though these Judaizers believed Jesus was their Messiah they did not want to break fellowship with Judaism. Wanting to make a good show in the flesh before the unbelieving Jews by capturing the churches of Galatia for Judaism, they compelled them to be circumcised.

2. **Fear of unbelieving Jews**. The Judaizers were believers that Jesus was the Christ. Otherwise they would not have been able to sneak in among the churches and voice their legalistic theology (2:4; Acts 15:5). But Paul tells us that their binding of circumcision on Gentile Christians was not motivated by a zeal to keep the law, but from a fear of persecution from unbelieving Jews. This fear produced in them the same kind of hypocrisy and inconsistency that it produced in Peter at Antioch (2:11-14). Paul further states that it compromised the gospel by doing away with the scandal of the cross. But if the cross implies the abolition of the law as necessary for salvation, and it does, then that eliminates circumcision as necessary for salvation. If these Judaizers preached the gospel of the cross they would not compel circumcision and that would mean war with the Jews as surely as Paul had experienced it. Their theology, in spite of their belief in Jesus as Lord, mitigated any ability they might otherwise have had to face the consequences of preaching the cross, as did Paul. Their real motives emerge in the practice of their hypocrisy: they were using believers in Christ at Galatia to establish a neutral zone for themselves in the camp of unbelievers!

3. **The Judaizers are inconsistent**. They bind circumcision but do not themselves keep the law, says Paul (Galatians 6:13). James

tells us that "whoever keeps the whole law and yet stumbles in one point, he has become guilty of all" (James 2:10). To bind one part of the law as necessary for salvation and at the same time disregard the rest of the law is inconsistent and hypocritical. Consequently if they were not keeping the rest of the law, and Paul indicates they were not, then their circumcision was of no value (cf. Romans 2:25) Their doctrine was thus inconsistent with both the gospel and the law, and their practice was hypocritically motivated. This argumentation should have convinced the Galatians of the genuine lack of sincerity the Judaizers had for their salvation, and should have exonerated Paul of the claims of hypocrisy made against him (as in Galatians 5:11).

C. THE CROSS IS THE SOLE GROUND FOR THE CHRISTIAN'S SALVATION AND CONFIDENCE, 6:14-16

1. **The cross is the Christian's ground for boasting**. One boasts in his confidence. The cross is the sole ground for the Christian's right standing with God. It is the Christian's glory inasmuch as it is God's guarantee that he has been freed from sin to remain free from sin. It is the Christian's confidence. Therefore, "far be it from me to glory, save in the cross of our Lord Jesus Christ" (ASV).

2. **The cross crucifies the world to me.** The world does not like me anymore than I like it. The gospel produces tension among unbelievers. "Do you suppose that I came to grant peace on earth? I tell you, no, but rather division" (Luke 12:51).

3. **The cross produces a new creation**. Through the cross we die to sin and self. By faith we turn ourselves over to the living Christ and walk by the Spirit's guidance into a new life that is grounded in a new foundation and motivated by a new and eternal hope. Behold all things are new (2 Corinthians 5:17).

4. **Those who walk by this rule**. The clear intent of the new birth is written throughout the New Testament: death to sin leads to our agreement to walk a new course of life according to the terms of a new covenant into which we entered with Christ at baptism. In this epistle Paul has already elaborated this rule as

cause and effect: "I have been crucified with Christ; and it is no longer I who live, but Christ lives in me; and the life which I now live in the flesh I live by faith in the Son of God (2:20)....If we live by the Spirit, let us also walk by the Spirit" (5:25). This is faith's condition for ongoing justification, as John once again reminds us, "If we walk in the Light...the blood of Jesus His Son cleanses us from all sin" (1 John 1:7). This course is not arbitrary; it's in keeping with God's original purpose for His creation to reflect the image of his Creator, as did Jesus who gave us the example (cf Romans 8:29). This radical change of lifestyle stands in opposition to those who would wear the crown but won't bear the cross.

5. **Peace and mercy.** The invaluable possessions, which continues to elude unbelievers precisely because of their lack of trust in Christ, is first, the peace that faithful Christians have precisely because of their trust in Christ as Lord and Savior. World peace is not under consideration here. This is peace with God which the world just cannot give (Romans 5:1; Ephesians 2:14; John 14:27). World peace, if it could be attained, could not erase the agonizing imaginations of the retribution that God has said He will inflict upon "those who do not know God and to those who do not obey the gospel...who will pay the penalty of eternal destruction away from the presence of the Lord and from the glory of his power" (2 Thessalonians 1:8-9). Faithful Christians have immediate access to the peace that guards both hearts and thoughts from the tyranny of a world in chaos and moral disentegration (Philippians 4:6-7). The Christian's confidence for now and for eternity is based on a right relationship with God that became ours when faith in Christ led to repentance and baptism for the remission of sins. And second, we are continually granted mercy for our sins while we maintain an obedience of faith with Christ (cf. Romans 9:23, 24; Titus 3:4-5). SALVATION

6. **And upon the Israel of God**. Paul does not speak of "Israel after the flesh" (1 Corinthians 10:18, ASV) as the true Israel of God. He does speak of Jews who are Jews inwardly, that is,

those who served God, not simply according to the letter of the law, but by the Spirit, from the heart (Romans 2:28-29). These Jews are identified as the true Jews whom God intended to represent Him prior to the cross. This statement in Galatians, being the only letter where he speaks of "the Israel of God," must be understood in keeping with the message of the epistle. Jews who become Christians are the true Israel of prophecy who were to be redeemed out of bondage. "For they are not all Israel who are descended from Israel....That is, it is not the children of the flesh who are children of God, but the children of the promise are regarded as descendants" (Romans 9:6-8). Paul reminds the Galatians that God made the promise to Abraham that from his seed, his descendant, would come a world-wide blessing embracing all nations (Genesis 12:3; 22:18). He then revealed that the Seed of that promise is Christ (Galatians 3:16) and that the promised blessing is justification by faith in Christ (Galatians 3:8). Thus all Israelites, even as all Gentiles, by faith in Christ become true sons of Abraham, for "if ye are Christ's then are ye Abraham's seed," whether Jew or Gentile (Galatians 3:29, ASV). But Israelites by faith in Christ become "the people of God," the Israel of prophecy, says Peter, who interprets it to Christian Jews of the Dispersion, who, though "once were not a people, but now you are the people of God" (1 Peter 2:10), fulfilling the prophecy by Hosea (1:10; 2:23; cf Romans 9:22-26). Here we have Israelites who by faith have become the people of God, the Israel of God. They have jettisoned law for grace, legalism for gospel, condemnation for mercy.

D. THE BRAND-MARKS OF CHRIST, 6:17

Paul bore upon his body the scars of persecution and hardship for the cross of Christ. These were proof of his integrity and commitment to Christ.

1. **Let no man trouble me.** The marks, which Paul labeled, "the brand-marks of Jesus," quieted the accusations that he preached the gospel for ulterior motives.

2. **I bear on my body the brand-marks of Jesus**. Without a doubt these brand-marks were scars left from the persecutions by stoning, beatings, and imprisonment (cf. Acts 14:19; 16:22-24; 2 Corinthians 11:22-30). From *stigmata* comes "stigma," a term of disgrace, a mark of reproach. One has suggested that this is a reference to the branding of slaves as a sign of owner-ship.[1] "This custom to mark slaves by scars - produced by cuts, prevented from closing as they healed, so as to leave broad wounds....The same custom existed in the country from ancient times. It was practiced on the temple slaves from time imme-morial; and the Galatian slave owners practiced it on their slaves."[2] Whether this is what Paul had in mind it is clear that Paul was indeed the slave of another, purchased by the cross and owned by Christ (1 Corinthians 6:19-20). Paul's point ap-pears to be that these scars in his body identify him as an un-compromising preacher of the truth of the gospel and one whose integrity in service to Christ is unimpeachable.

IV. A Christian Wish For All Believers, 6:19

Every letter written by the apostle Paul opens and closes with a sin-cere reference to the grace of Christ as a wished-for blessing upon his read-ers. From what we now know about the saving, healing, strengthening grace of God in Christ, what greater, more needful blessing could be wished upon anyone? Paul closes the Galatian letter.

CONCLUSION: Paul finalizes his letter by appealing to the practical-ity of freedom's walk by the Spirit in brotherly love. He concludes with a graphic twofold contrast of the true motives behind the Judaizers' purpose for seeking out the Galatians and his own, and their respective objects of glory and confidence: theirs the flesh, Paul's the cross.

Spiritual Probing
Chapter Thirteen

1. Paul said that spiritual brethren are to restore those who are caught up in trespasses. Define the spiritual brother. Define the brother who is not spiritual. Now explain why only spiritual brethren should attempt to restore fallen brethren.

2. Brethren who are hyper-critical, always finding fault with something or someone, probably fit the description of the person in Galatians 6:3. What do you think? How could such a brother or sister be approached for the long-term healing that is required?

3. What is the law of Christ in Galatians 6:2? How is it fulfilled?

4. Do you feel a personal indebtedness to those who minister the Word of God to you to the extent you are willing to give of your income so they can have an adequate income? Look at Luke 8:1-3 and 1 Corinthians 9:1-16 as a commentary on Galatians 6:6-10.

5. Take a close look at Galatians 6:11. It stands in stark contrast to the ministry motives of the false teachers expressed in Galatians 6:12, 13. How does this statement reflect Paul's ministry motives? Galatians 4:15, 19, 20 can help you answer.

6. We say that the cross is the sole ground of the Christian's salvation and confidence. That is absolutely true. What is there about the cross that undergirds that statement? Is the cross of Christ your glory? What does it mean to you personally to glory in the cross?

7. We know that the cross crucifies Christians to the world. How does the cross crucify the world to Christians (Galatians 6:14)?

8. How does the cross produce a new creature (Galatians 6:15)? 9. What is the "rule" of Galatians 6:16?

9. What were the brand-marks that Paul bore in his flesh (Galatians 6:17)?

10. Why did he mention the brand-marks? In answering, consider the following: the Judaizers were causing trouble for Paul (Galatians 5:11). They were maligning his character and his ministry motives;

they were persecuting him for preaching the cross inasmuch as the cross did away with the law. But he would not compromise either the gospel or his convictions by preaching circumcision to keep the Jews off his back. Paul was a man of reliable Christian integrity, yet his integrity was being challenged. Those brand-marks confirmed his integrity to the Galatians and silenced his accusers. Would you explain how?

11. According to Galatians 1:3 and 6:18 what would be one of the most meaningful greetings, salutations, and Christian wishes that one Christian could wish for another? Why?

Endnotes

Chapter One

[1] See Bruce's *New International Greek Testament Commentary on Galatians*, pp. 5-10, and Hendriksen's *Epistle To the Galatians*, pp. 4-14, for a more thorough presentation of the views on the northern versus the southern Galatian theories.

[2] Ilasting's *Dictionary Of the Bible* (New York: Charles Scribner's Sons, 1952), p. 510.

[3] Leon Morris, *The Apostolic Preaching Of the Cross* (Grand Rapids: William B. Eerdmans Publishing Co., 1976), p. 224.

[4] Glenn Owens, "Galatians: Gospel of Grace," Christian Adult Series, Highland church of Christ, Abilene, Texas (1984), lesson 6, p. 10.

[5] Morris, p. 247.

[6] Owens, lesson 1, p. 11.

Chapter Two

[1] Robert Gundry, *A Survey Of the New Testament* (Grand Rapids: 7Amdervan, 1970), p. 257. (Quoted from Glenn Owens, "Galatians: Gospel Of Grace," lesson 2, page 2.)

[2] Henry Alford, *The Greek Testament*, vol. III (Cambridge: Deighton, Bell, and Co., 1865), p. 64.

[3] William Barclay, *The Letters To the Galatians and Ephesians* (Edinburgh: The Saint Andrews Press, 1965), pp. xiv, xv.

Chapter Three

[1] F.F. Bruce, *New Testament Documents: Are They Reliable?* (Grand Rapids: William B. Eerdmans Publishing Co., 1960), p.82.

[2] Merrill C. Tenney, *Galatians, The Charter Of Christian Liberty* (Grand Rapids: William B.Eerdmans Publishing Co., 1954), pp. 84, 85.

[3] Bruce, *New Testament Documents*, p. 77.

[4] R.C. Bell, *Studies In Galatians* (Austin: Firm Foundation Publishing House, 1954), p. 12.

[5] F.F. Bruce, *New International Greek Testament Commentary, The Epistle To the Galatians* (Grand Rapids: William B. Eerdmans Publishing Co., 1982), p.21.

Chapter Five

[1] Maxie B. Dunnam, *The Communicator's Commentary*, vol. 8 (Dallas: Word Publishing, 1982), p.42.

[2] Frank E. Gaebelein, *The Expositor's Bible Commentary* (Grand Rapids: Zondervan, 1975), p. 452. (Quoted by Glenn Owens, Galatians: Gospel Of Grace, lesson 7) p. 14.

Chapter Six

[1] Paul does not call the New Testament the letter of the law, nor does he say that to abide by the teaching of Christ under the new covenant is legalistic. In 2 Corinthians 3:1-7, Paul clearly refers to the law of Moses as "the letter" that "kills." Because of its threefold legal nature, the law of Moses is called what it is—a ministration of condemnation and death. Paul places the Mosaic system in contrast to the new covenant that is written on men's hearts. The letter that kills is the legal system of Moses, not the written word of the New Testament from which we deduce the terms of the new covenant given for our justification.

[3] Bruce, *New International Greek Testament Commentary*, p. 164. Owens, lesson 8, p. 12.

[4] It is interesting to note that Peter teaches that remission of sins and the gift of the Holy Spirit are by repentance and baptism (Acts 2:38). What, then, is baptism but the expression of our faith in Christ to save us when He said He would? Jesus paid the price of our deliverance on the cross "that he might redeem us from every lawless deed and purify for himself a people for his own possession" (Titus 2:14). But we are baptized into Christ's possession (Matthew 28:19; Acts 8:14; 19:5; 1 Corinthians 1:13, where the translation "into the name of" means "into the possession of").

"In the Greek papyri, 'Into the name' was 'a common phrase for transference of ownership'" (Stephen L. Caiger, *Archaeology and the New Tes-*

tament [London: Cassell and Co., 19481, p. 164. Adolph Deissmann, *Light From the Ancient East* New York: George H. Doran Co., 19271, p. 21. Adolph Deissmann, *Biblical Studies* 'Edinburgh: T. and 1'. Clark, 19091, pp. 146, 147. George Milligan, *The Vocabulary of the Greek New Testament* [Grand Rapids: William B. Eerdmans Publishing Co., 19541, p. 451, as quoted by James D. Bales, *The Case Of Cornelius* [Delight, AR: Gospel Light Publishing Co., 19641, pp. 84, 85). Bales observes from this base that "baptism into the name indicates that one belongs to the one into whose name he is baptized. In baptism we are baptized into the name of the Father, the Son and the Holy Spirit. We enter into their possession."

Chapter Seven

[1] Willis Judson Beecher, *The Prophets and the Promise* (Grand Rapids: Baker Book House, 1963), pp. 176-178.

[2] For a discussion of the meaning of the Hebrew word for seed see William Hendriksen's *Epistle to the Galatians*, pp. 133-137.

[3] "...a slave, whose duty it was to conduct the youth to and from school and to superintend his conduct gener.; he was not 'a teacher' (despite the present mng. of the derivative 'pedagogue'...When the young man became of age the 'paidagogos' was no longer needed." Arndt and Gingrich, *A Greek-English Lexicon Of the New Testament* (Chicago: University of Chicago Press, 1952), p. 608.

[4] W.E. Vine, *Expository Dictionary of New Testament Words* (Old Tappan, NJ: Fleming H. Revell Co., 1959), p. 265.

[5] *The New Bible Commentary: Revised* (Grand Rapids: William B. Eerdmans Publishing Co., 1978), p. 1099.

[6] This indwelling gift of the Spirit should not be confused with the empowering of the Holy Spirit that was given to some first-century Christians. Acts 19:6 says And when Paul had laid his hands upon them, the Holy Spirit came on them, and they began speaking with tongues and prophesying." It is debated whether Paul refers to the indwelling Spirit or the empowering of the Spirit when he asks the Ephesians "Did you receive the Holy Spirit when you believed?" (Acts 19:2). In either, case, the Spirit would not be given either to indwell or empower until after baptism by faith in Christ to save.

7 Donald Guthrie, *The New Century Bible Commentary, Galatians* (Grand Rapids: William B. Eerdmans Publishing Co., 1981), p. 110.

8 Herman R. Ridderbos, *The Epistle of Paul to the Churches of Galatia* (Grand Rapids: William B. Eerdmans Publishing Co., 1965), pp. 147, 148.

9 H.D. McDonald, *Freedom In Faith* (Old Tappan, NJ: Fleming H. Revell Co., 1946), pp. 88, 89. (Quoted from Glenn Owens, Galatians: Gospel Of Grace, lesson 11) p. 5.

10 *The Interpreter's Bible*, vol. 10 (New York: Abingdon Press, 1957), pp. 519, 520.

Chapter Eight

1 Bruce, *New International Greek Testament Commentary*, pp. 193, 194.

2 Guthrie, p. 113.

Chapter Nine

1 William M. Ramsay, *A Historical Commentary on St. Paul's Epistle to the Galatians* (Grand Rapids: Baker Book House, 1979), p. 323.

2 Bell, p. 1.

3 Ramsay, pp. 422-425.

4 Ben Witherington III, *Grace In Galatia*, p.311.

5 Ridderbos, p. 167.

6 Witherington, pp. 311-312.

7 Guthrie, p. 120.

8 Witherington, pp. 9-10.

Chapter Ten

1 R.C.H. Lenski, *The Interpretation of St. Paul's Epistles to the Galatians, to the Ephesians, and to the Philippians* (Columbus, OH: Wartburg Press, 1937), p. 239.

Chapter Eleven

1 Bruce, *New International Greek Testament Commentary*, p. 231.

2 Ibid.

Chapter Twelve

[1] Charles Cousar, *Interpretation of Galatians* (Atlanta: John Knox Press, 1982), p. 122.

Chapter Thirteen

[1] Donald Guthrie quoting William Ramsay, *The New Century Bible Commentary*, p. 152.

[2] William Ramsay, *A Historical Commentary on St. Paul's Epistle to the Galatians*,(Baker Book House) pp 472-473.

Selected Bibliography

Alford, Henry. *The Greek Testament*, Vol. III. Cambridge: Deighton, Bell, and Co., 1865.

Barclay, William. *The Letters to the Galatians and Ephesians*. Edinburgh: The Saint Andrew Press, 1965.

Beecher, Willis Judson. *The Prophets and the Promise*. (Grand Rapids: Baker Book House, 1963.

Bell, R.C. *Studies in Galatians*. Austin: The Firm Foundation Publishing House, 1954.

Blackwelder, Oscar F. and Raymond T. Stamm. *The Interpreter's Bible*, Voila New York: Abingdon Press, 1953.

Brown, John. *The Epistle of Paul the Apostle to the Galatians*. Minneapolis: Klock & Mock Christian Publishers Inc., 1957.

Bruce, F.F. *New International Greek Testament Commentary*, Galatians. Grand Rapids: William B. Eerdmans Publishing Co., 1982.

Colson, Howard P. and Robert J. Dean. *Galatians: Freedom Through Christ*. Nashville: Convention Press, 1972.

Cousar, Charles B. *Interpretation of Galatians*. Atlanta: John Knox Press, 1982.

Decker, Bill. "*The Early Dating of Galatians*." Restoration Quarterly, 2, No. 3. (1958).

Dunnam, Maxie D. *The Communicator's Commentary*, Vol. 8. Dallas: Word Publishing, 1982.

Eerdmans, Charles, R. *The Epistle of Paul to the Galatians*. Philadelphia: The Westminster Press.

Fischer, John. *"Messianic Midrash, Survey of Galatians."* Congregational Roeh Israel, (1993).

Govett, Robert. *Govett on Galatians*. Miami Springs: Conley & Schoettle Publishing Co., 1981.

Guthrie, Donald. *The New Century Bible Commentary*. Grand Rapids: William B. Eerdmans Pub. Co., 1973.

Hendriksen, William. *A Commentary on Galatians*. London: The Banner of Truth, 1968.

Jones, Jerry. *From Slavery to Sonship*. Nashville: Christian Communications, 1989.

Jervis, L. Ann, *GALATIANS*, New International Biblical Commentary, Hendrickson Publishers.

Lenski, R.C.H. , *The Interpretation of St. Paul's Epistles to the Galatians, to the Ephesians, and to the Philippians*. Columbus, OH: Wartburg Press, 1937.

Lightfoot, J.B. *St. Paul's Epistle to the Galatians*. Peabody: Hendrickson Publishers, 1981.

Luther, Martin. *A Commentary on Saint Paul's Epistle to the Galatians*. Grand Rapids: Baker Book House. Reprinted 1979.

Morris, Leon. *The Apostolic Preaching of the Cross*. Grand Rapids: William B. Eerdmans Pub. Co., 1955.

Moser, K. C. *Galatians*. Austin: R.B. Sweet Co., 1965.

Owen, Glenn. *Galatians: Gospel of Grace*. Christian Adult Series, Highland Church of Christ, Abilene, Texas, 1984

Ramsay, William M. A, *Historical Commentary on St. Paul's Epistle to the Galatians*. Grand Rapids: Baker Book House. Reprinted 1979.

Ramsay, William. *St. Paul the Traveler and the Roman Citizen*, Grand Rapids, Baker Book House. Reprinted 1982.

Ridderbos, Herman N. *The Epistle of Paul to the Churches of Galatia*. Grand Rapids: William B. Eerdmans Pub. Co., 1965.

Tenney, Merrill C. Galatians: *The Charter of Christian Liberty*. Grand Rapids: William B. Eerdmans Pub. Co., 1954

Thompson, James. *Preaching From Galatians*. Paper from 1983 Sermon Seminar at Abilene Christian University (for information for reprints contact the author at Abilene Christian University).

Swindoll, Charles R. *Letter of Liberation*. Waco: Word Publishing Co., 1981.

Vine, W.E. *Expository Dictionary Of New Testament Words*. (Old Tappan, NJ: Fleming H. Revell Co., 1978.

Wiersbe, Warren W. *Be Free*. Wheaton: Victor Books, Scripture Press Publications, 1989.

Witherington III, Ben, *GRACE IN GALATIA: A Commentary on Paul's Letter to the Galatians,* Wm. B. Eerdmans, 1998.